Images from Science 2

An Exhibition of Scientific Photography

Images from Science 2

An Exhibition of Scientific Photography

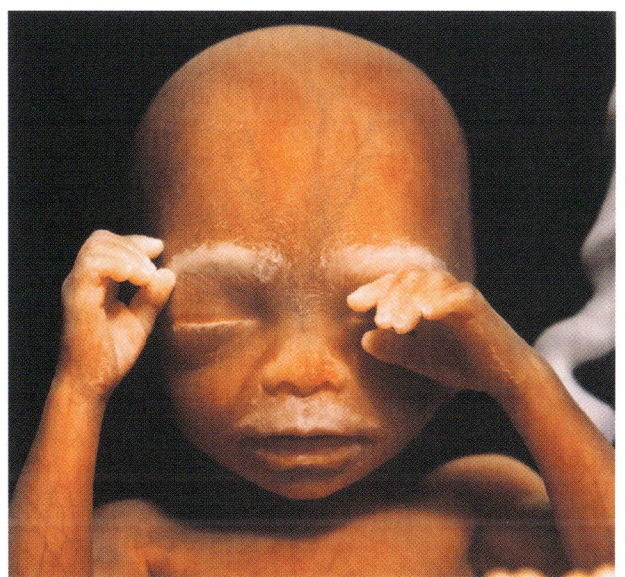

Organized by the RIT School of Photographic Arts and Sciences

RIT Cary Graphic Arts Press
Rochester, New York
2008

Images from Science 2: An Exhibition of Scientific Photography
http://images.rit.edu

Published and distributed by
RIT Cary Graphic Arts Press
90 Lomb Memorial Drive
Rochester, New York 14623
http://carypress.rit.edu

Cover photograph: David Paul, Victoria, Australia, *Octopus Paralarvae, 2000*

Title page: Lennart Nilsson, *Six month old Fetus Revealing Lanugo*
Karolinska Institutet Stockholm, Sweden
This photograph was made of a human fetus barely 6 months of age. Specialized approaches and lighting were used to highlight the matted lanugo, which forms interesting patterns and reveals how the oblique roots of the hair are positioned in the skin. This image is part of a much larger body of work the photographer has produced exploring life before birth beginning at conception for more than 50 years.

Printed in the United States
ISBN 978-1-933360-34-8

Library of Congress Cataloging-in-Publication Data

Images from science 2 : an exhibition of scientific photography / organized by the RIT School of Photographic Arts and Sciences.
     p. cm.
  ISBN 978-1-933360-34-8 (alk. paper)
 1. Photography—Scientific applications—Exhibitions. I. Rochester Institute of Technology. School of Photographic Arts and Sciences.
 TR692.I4332 2008
 779--dc22
                                                                              2008036981

Contents

Foreword

Photography courses were first offered at the Rochester Institute of Technology in 1902. The production of the *Images from Science 2* project is a fitting tribute to more than 100 years of photographic activities in this university. The School of Photographic Arts and Sciences has had a rich history of contributions to photographic education and exploration during this time.

This project is one more example of many significant achievements that have come out of this school and its faculty. The imagination that led to *Images from Science 2* could only have come from individuals who are committed to excellence in photographic arts and sciences. RIT and the College of Imaging Arts and Sciences in particular, are proud to be associated with the important and beautiful work represented in this exhibition. On behalf of the university, I want to thank Professor Andrew Davidhazy and Professor Michael Peres for their impressive achievement.

Dr. Joan Stone
Dean, College of Imaging Arts and Sciences
Rochester Institute of Technology

Preface

In October 2002, the *Images from Science* exhibition opened at the SPAS gallery at Rochester Institute of Technology, Rochester, New York. The goal for that exhibition was to provide a venue for showcasing exceptional photographs that were rarely seen outside of the scientific, technological, or engineering disciplines in which they were originally created.

We acknowledged that exhibitions of creative and artistic photographs were common and that our society at large was very aware of the impact of photography in the art world. We were not so sure that the contributions of photographs made for scientific, medical, or technological purposes would have a similar level of recognition either in the art or the scientific communities. Our first *Images from Science* exhibition was designed to explore this and other issues.

By way of background, we should explain that with a very small initial operating budget we had to devise methods for soliciting the contributions, mounting the exhibition and producing ancillary materials such as a catalogue. To do this, we used the Internet to be the principal promotional tool for the project because we hoped we would gain participation from a global audience. The Internet was efficient and low cost. Using the Internet would also provide us new and useful experiences in determining the "limitations" of this new communications technology.

When we began this experiment in 2001, things were different and there have been numerous changes in the world of photography and applied imaging in general since that time. This has resulted in major advances in imaging processes and technologies, especially in the area of digital imaging. Further, the number of applied, scientific, and technical image-makers has grown significantly as a direct consequence of these changes. Because of these factors we decided to mount a second *Images from Science* exhibition. We feel this new edition reflects many of the new imaging processes and techniques that were not possible just a few years ago.

In scientific photography more than in other types of photography, there is the constant struggle for new discovery, which drives new activities. The following pages feature stunning work drawn from the broadest definition of science including oceanography, geology, biology, engineering, medicine, and physics. These photographs are not only appealing visualizations of seldom seen events, but also they are rich with significant scientific data.

As was the strategy for our first project, *Images from Science 2* was advertised to a worldwide audience in the following manner.

> Organized to showcase photographs made in the pursuit of science, *Images from Science 2* welcomes photographs made with any imaging tool as the source, not only traditional photographic ones. This invitation, the exhibition's solicitation for entries and the process of image contribution, etc. will be conducted primarily using the Internet. We would appreciate you sharing this announcement with others to accomplish our goal of developing this international exhibition.

> Acceptance into this juried show will be based on the photograph's impact, the image's aesthetics, the degree of difficulty in the making of the photograph, as well as other related criteria. A maximum of 4 images may be submitted by any given individual for selection consideration.

When the submission phase for *Images from Science 2* was over, more than 315 images, from 103 photographers representing 12 countries were received for consideration.

As we did in the first installation, we again decided to include a guest essay as an introduction to the exhibition and enlisted the help of Martin Scott, the former director of scientific imaging at Eastman Kodak, to help us in this task. We also invited an international group of judges to work with us and they also used the Internet as a judging platform. Judges were selected to represent a wide range of backgrounds from the field that included: scientists, scientific photographers, and educators, practicing artists, as well as photography editors. Each judge received the following instructions.

Select 75 images.

> We believe that this number of votes when distributed across 7 judges will create enough overall "voting emphasis" to allow the selection of approximately 50 of the best images.

> No more than 2 entries per person can be in the final list of qualifying entries. This is important for the project to establish a diverse exhibition. If in the judging outcomes, one individual exceeds more than two selections, the project coordinators will eliminate the image(s) with the least amount of votes.

Choose one entry for guaranteed inclusion.

> The organizers want to provide an opportunity for each judge to select one image for automatic inclusion into the exhibition.

Sixty-one photographs were ultimately selected for inclusion in the exhibition.

In summary, we are indebted to all of the early pioneers of scientific photography who paved the road for today's image-makers and who dedicated their lives to making photographs in difficult and seemingly impossible situations. For this exhibition, we again invited Lennart Nilsson to contribute one of his photographs not only as a tribute to his importance as a pioneer scientific photographer, but equally because he has worked tirelessly to make images in places people can't go without knowledge, curiosity, and instrumentation.

We would like to thank our collaborators in this work whose aesthetic and scientific achievements made this exhibition and catalogue possible. We thank them for trusting us with their images. In closing, we hope that you enjoy the *Images from Science 2* exhibition as much as we enjoyed producing it.

Professor Andrew Davidhazy
Chair, Imaging and Photographic Technology
School of Photographic Arts and Sciences
Rochester Institute of Technology

Professor Michael Peres
Chair, Biomedical Photographic Communications
School of Photographic Arts and Sciences
Rochester Institute of Technology

June 2008

Introduction: Images for Science

As minds explore the workings of the world and the universe, words alone are often inadequate to describe new discoveries and knowledge. In these circumstances images supplement words. The ancient Chinese proverb about the value of a picture is a vast underestimation. Indeed, in many cases no finite number of words can express the information a photograph can convey. Science has always been intertwined with images.

Early astronomers chiseled on stone plazas the daily progression of a gnomon's shadow to determine the solstices and to measure the sun's annual motion. They sketched charts of the wanderings of the planets against the background of fixed stars, eventually deducing the laws of planetary motion. Euclid (ca. 300 BC) scratched his triangles and circles in the sand as he taught geometry to his school. Leonardo da Vinci (1452–1519) sketched the moons of Saturn and the sinews of the human body for incredulous nobility. In the 17th century, Robert Hooke (1635–1703) in England and Anton von Leeuwenhoek (1632–1723) in Holland, were seeing marvelous things using their primitive microscopes. Actually seeing with these early instruments was not easy, and repeated attempts at observation required great patience and greater skill. How could they convince others of what they were seeing—the microbes in a drop of water, the wing scales of butterflies, the facets of a fly's eye? Hooke was quite good at sketching what he saw, but Leeuwenhoek had no such talent, and needed to describe his observations to an artist who made the drawings. It is amazing that such an arrangement could have resulted in images that stand the test of today's observations with modern instruments.

Scientists have always needed to communicate their discoveries with each other. In science it is necessary to repeat each other's findings to validate or disprove claims of new knowledge. To do this requires publication and worldwide distribution. While early photographs of scientific phenomena provided the original image, there was no way to get that image onto the printed page in a scientific journal for mass distribution. The printing methods of the 19th century could not handle the range of tones from white to black with all the intermediate gradations. Presses could only print black ink or nothing on the white paper. Engravers took the original photograph or sketch from the scientist, and line by line, scribed it into a printing plate. Days were sometimes consumed to make a single illustration. It is no wonder that early scientific books had few pictures. Eventually imaging scientists solved these problems. Around 1900 the optical scientist Frederic Eugene Ives (1856–1937) cleverly used optical means to convert continuous tone photographs into millions of vanishingly small dots of varying sizes, enabling the printing press to produce a simulation of continuous tone. Newspapers and magazines still use a variant of this process, as does this book.

But that is getting ahead of the story. As scientific knowledge grew, science eventually provided the means to make its own images. In the late 1700s, Karl Wilhelm Scheele (1742–1786) discovered that a slurry of silver chloride darkened upon exposure to light. This phenomenon had extremely feeble sensitivity by today's standards; it took hours of exposure to sunlight to make the image of a stencil. It would be another seventy years before chemists would find a way to amplify a minimal exposure to light to produce a visible image. Even these first images would fade if viewed in room light. Another chemist would find a way to make the fugitive images impervious to further exposure to light. Achievements in optics combined with chemical advances to become basis of practical photography. With little fundamental knowledge to guide them, early experimenters tried even the most improbable things. Who would have thought that light could make images with asphalt and oil of lavender?

Early photography in the 19th century was more art than science, and very dangerous art at that. Louis-Jacques-Mandé Daguerre (1781–1851) in France treated his plates of silver with the vapors of iodine and bromine, the fumes of hot mercury, and solutions of potassium cyanide to make his exquisite images in 1839. Today's safety watchdogs would be aghast at the use of those deadly poisons. Beautiful as the Daguerreotype process was, each exposure gave only a single image, which could not be easily or accurately copied. William Henry Fox Talbot (1800–1877) in England, working at the same time as Daguerre, invented another silver halide process that yielded an image in which tones were reversed—lights were dark, shadows were bright. By copying this negative image to another sensitive sheet, natural tones were restored. Any number of positive images could easily be made from the original. From this process all subsequent silver processes have sprung.

Light sensitivity is a property of several elements or their compounds: iron, mercury, selenium, silver, to name a few. One element alone possesses this property to a supreme degree—silver. Compounds of silver with a halogen—the elements chlorine, bromine, and iodine—have the ability to remember a brief exposure to the image projected by the lens of a camera. That memory can be awakened by chemical processing to take this invisible "latent image," and amplify it to a very visible, permanent picture. This silver halide process dominated photography for one hundred and fifty years. Originally it made pictures in shades of gray, but by mid-20th century chemical research brought full color snapshots and movies within the budgets of almost everyone.

Early photographic experimenters had little scientific understanding to build on. Would a splash of beer, or a dollop of honey improve a silver halide emulsion? Would extracts of plant leaves and blossoms? Would boiling increase sensitivity? One early emulsion maker found that eating a raw onion for lunch, then adding his urine to the emulsion made a great improvement in sensitivity. (It would be decades until the chemical reason for this would be discovered.) Once in the 1880s when batch after batch of emulsion failed to work, desperate George Eastman (1854–1932) called his workers to a meeting to pray for the emulsion. Hiring a good chemist eventually proved to be more reliable than divine intervention. Improvements accelerated when university-trained scientists eventually replaced intuitive experimenters.

The sciences of theoretical and applied chemistry promoted early photography from a slow, tedious, failure-prone, trial-and-error process to its ultimate technological triumph. This mention of chemistry should remind us that images born in chemistry will die in chemistry unless prevented by intelligent conservation techniques. Here science is again serving image-making through ongoing studies of image conservation at universities and museums. This back-and-forth cooperation of scientists and image-makers continues to the advantage of all who make, or use, or enjoy images.

In the mid-19th century scientists quickly took up this new tool—photography— and applied it to the microscope, to the telescope, to the spectroscope. Archeologists, explorers, and ethnographers put cameras in their field kits. Later, through the use of motion pictures, scientists were able to stretch and shrink time to study extremely rapid phenomena—the flight of a bullet—or the very slow—the growth of plant roots and the movement of glaciers. Data gathering was greatly speeded up. To measure the magnitude (brightness) of a single star using visual methods at the telescope required several minutes. A single photographic plate could record the magnitudes of hundreds of stars in one exposure.

Astronomers rate the intensity of starlight in terms of a magnitude scale. (Contrary to intuition, the greater the magnitude, the dimmer the star.) Each unit of magnitude represents a factor of about 2.5 in brightness. On a good night, the dark-adapted human eye can see stars of magnitude about 6.5. The digital sensors of the Hubble Telescope staring for long exposure times can see objects fainter than magnitude 30. That's over two and a half trillion times fainter than a human can see. The aptly named OWL Telescope (Overwhelmingly Large Telescope) now in the planning stage is expected to see to the 38th magnitude. Only electronic sensors, not human eyes or silver halide plates, will ever receive its images. The astronomer need not even be present at the telescope when the images he has requested are being acquired. He may be in his office half a world away, "seeing" through OWL on his computer screen.

Scientists need new tools to study new fields. They rely on imaging scientists for help. Biologists ask optical scientists for microscopes capable of revealing finer details. Astronomers want telescopes with more power to grasp the feeble light of distant galaxies. Scientists of all stripes ask for detectors that are not limited to the visible spectrum, detectors that will lift faint signals from noisy backgrounds. Imaging scientists take up these challenges.

This interplay of science and image making was well understood by Dr. C. E. K. Mees, (1882–1960), Kodak's first director of research and holder of that position for over forty years. Great commercial success was gained by applying science to the invention of new photographic products. Paraphrasing Mees: "Science has been good to Photography, and Photography should be good to Science." Guided by that motto, he made many special films and emulsions for scientists with no regard for profitability. Indeed, many such materials were given to scientists free of charge. That all sounds very altruistic, but sometimes there were unexpected rewards. A technique learned while making a special emulsion for an astronomer was later adapted to produce one of the most successful films ever made for general photography, Kodak Tri-X. There were also non-tangible rewards from making special materials for Science. One special spectroscopic plate produced for astronomers doubled the size of the knowable universe at one stroke! The reward for that was the satisfaction and pride in literally advancing the frontiers of knowledge.

There is a difference in the manner in which human eyes and man-made sensors respond to light. After the first few minutes in very dim light, the eye becomes dark-adapted, and it sees things not at first visible when the lights went out. However, no amount of staring after that will reveal more. Chemical and electronic sensors can do better than that. The longer they stare, the more they can see. Unlike our eyes, they are able to continue to collect and store light. There is an old truism: "If you can see it, you can photograph it." Today an imaging scientist would add, "Even if you can't see it, you can probably photograph it."

Imaging scientists are most successful when the technology they develop for us is invisible to us. Much of our daily business depends on document copying. This is a function we all take for granted, not even thinking of it as a form of photography. The original Xerox copying machines depended on the light sensitivity of selenium. These machines are now digital. Looking back before Xerox in the history of the document copying field we find Photostat machines that used silver halide, also the blueprint process depending on the light sensitivity of iron compounds, and the whiteprint (blueline) process using diazonium compounds. Digital imaging here too has swept these earlier systems onto the junk pile.

The spectacular images of human's first venture to the Moon convinced American tax-payers that NASA's huge budget was worthwhile after all. Prior to that, Moon-orbiting cameras sent images that prepared the way for human landing. The citizenry came to love the Hubble Telescope after seeing its stunning views of beautiful galaxies, helping to save the instrument beyond its scheduled date for decommissioning. Cameras can go where humans have not yet been able to go, or will never go: thermal vents lying miles deep in the sea, the surfaces of Mars and the Moon. Cameras the size of a vitamin pill can be swallowed by sufferers with gastric diseases. These tiny cameras with built-in television transmitters send detailed images of the interior of the alimentary canal to tell surgeons exactly where the trouble lies.

The influence of scientific and technological imaging in our lives is staggering. Let's name some applications:

- The entire Earth is being mapped by satellite and low-altitude cameras to a degree of accuracy and detail impossible with land-based surveying.

- The core of each of today's electronic marvels is a computer chip that is actually manufactured solely by imaging processes—lenses projecting images on sensitive materials at extremely short ultraviolet wavelengths.

- The properties of nanostructures, claimed to be the wonder materials of coming technology, are studied mainly by electron microscope images.

- Molecular biology, using the images of fluorescence microscopy linked to intracellular molecules, is transforming our understanding of life itself.

- Jurisprudence relies increasingly on imaging technology to solve crimes and present evidence.

- Proof of identity through automatic fingerprint or retinal imaging seems soon to replace facial photographs for security purposes.

- Magnetic resonance imaging relates specific areas of the brain in real time to dynamic thought processes.

Using various imaging processes a scientist can detect or measure the position, orientation, color, temperature, speed, acceleration, chemical composition, state of health, distance, identity, internal structure, change-over-time, and other properties of the object he studies.

For over a hundred years the great versatility of silver diverted photographic manufacturers from exploring other light-sensitive materials. Scientists in computer firms had no such veneration of silver. They used computer-chip technology to produce light-sensitive arrays on silicon wafers. These charge-coupled devices (CCDs) have evolved over the last several decades to the point where they have almost totally replaced silver halide technology for many applications. These electronic imaging systems store their images digitally in computer memory chips for viewing on computer screens or for printing with ink-jet technology. The wet processing of silver halide materials is virtually extinct, practiced by a few fine-arts photographers. Most photography using microscopes and all astrophotography are now done with electronic sensors. Digital cameras are the overwhelming choice of amateur and professional photographers today. Most cellular phones contain digital cameras.

Are today's imaging scientists, caught up in applying electronic digital techniques, perhaps overlooking the next technology that could replace it? Could Nature's living biological imaging systems provide a key to an imaging system of the future? Will something undreamed of supplant today's systems? Open minds will answer that. It seems likely that science and image making will continue their mutually beneficial relationship.

Martin L. Scott

Mr. Scott is the former Director of Scientific Imaging for Eastman Kodak Company, where he enjoyed a long career helping scientists of all interests in finding solutions to their imaging problems. He has lectured widely on the critical use of the light microscope and he is a past president of the Biological Photographic Association, now the BioCommunications Association. He consults on image conservation at George Eastman House International Museum of Photography and Film in Rochester, New York. Other interests include the history of photography, early music, letterpress printing, collecting antique microscopes, and the English language as an aid to international understanding.

The Exhibition

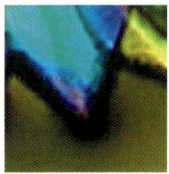

Donald Anthony

Citric Acid, 2004

Photomicrograph; Zeiss microscope with polarizing light filters;
Nikon 5000 digital camera

Peterborough, Ontario, Canada

Citric acid is a natural preservative that is found in citrus fruits or can be synthetically manufactured in the lab. It is often used to produce acidic or sour tastes in foods and soft drinks. For this photomicrograph, citric acid powder was dissolved in water and dried rapidly on a clear slide to form crystals. The crystals were then photographed using a microscope equipped with a series of polarizing filters that revealed the internal colors, or birefringence, associated with this compound when examined under polarized light. When energy is polarized, it is all oscillating in the same orientation. When two polarizing filters are oriented at 90 degrees to one another, all incident energy is subtracted from the system. When a material that contains multiple refractive indices is viewed in this system, the various components may appear as different colors.

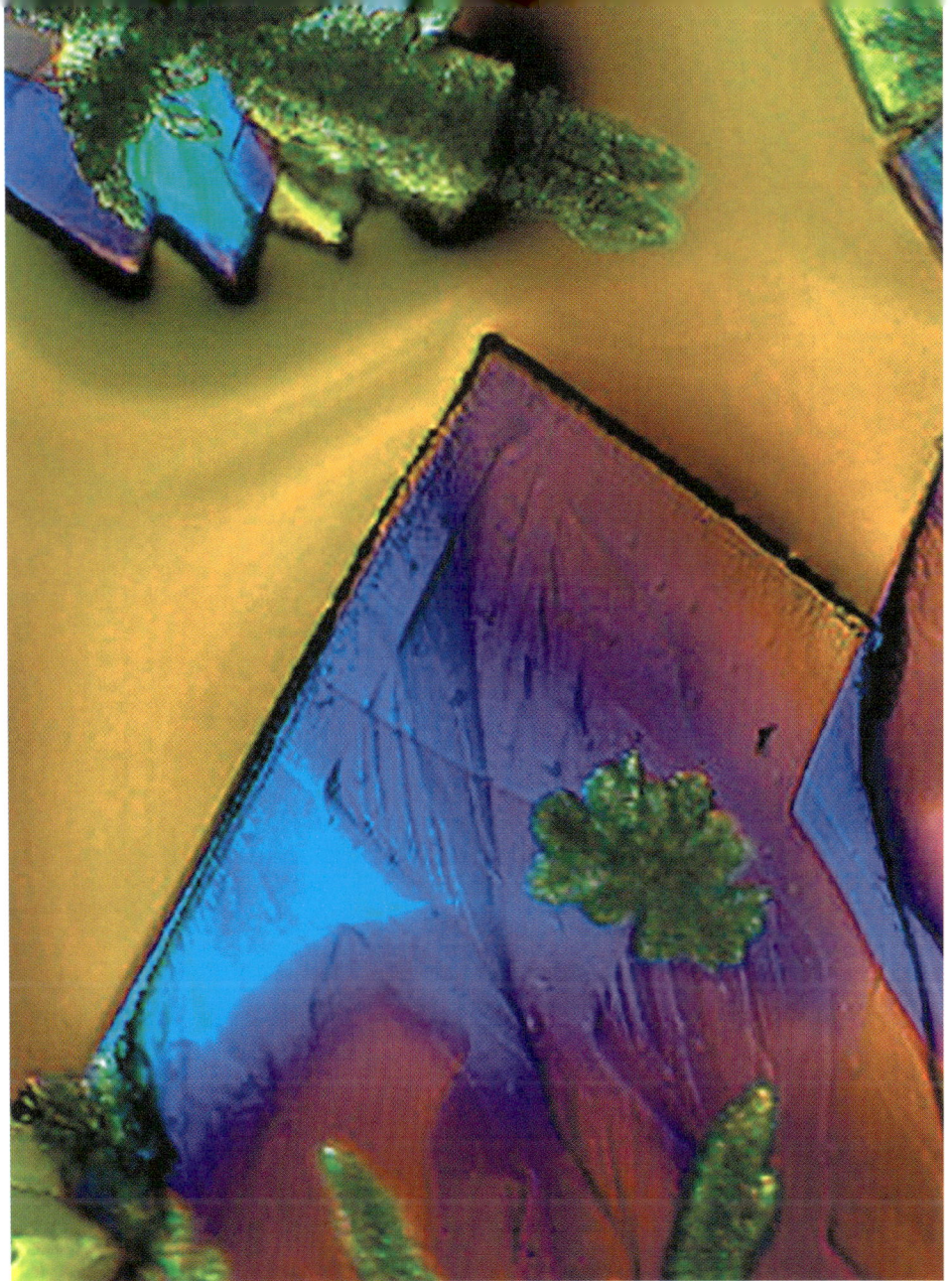

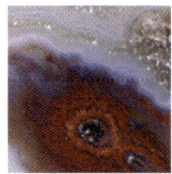

Norman Barker

Dinosaur Bone ×15, 2001

Photomicrograph; magnification approximately ×15 at capture;
Hasselblad camera, bellows, and 40 mm Zeiss Luminar lens; Kodak EPP Film

Johns Hopkins University, School of Medicine, Baltimore, Maryland, United States

There are specific structures that can be observed in bone fragments, which allows
for the determination as to whether they might have come from a dinosaur. One such
determining factor is the location where the bone was found. Initially, this sample was
found in the Morrison Formation in Colorado, where dinosaur remains are common.
The estimated age of this region, and the geologic formations there, corresponds to
the middle part of the dinosaur period—the Jurassic period. The most confirming
element of the analysis of these samples is that a dinosaur bone itself is five or six
times thicker than the largest adult male human long bone. That being shared,
this sample had to have come from a very large animal. Contrary to its appearance,
the red structure within the quartz-filled medullary cavity is not a nutrient artery.
Soft tissue rarely becomes fossilized, and when it does, it is rarely replaced by quartz.
The red color comes principally from hematite, an iron oxide. In the lower right of
this photomicrograph is the metaphyseal bone, also called spongy bone, with blue
chalcedony visible between the spicules.

4

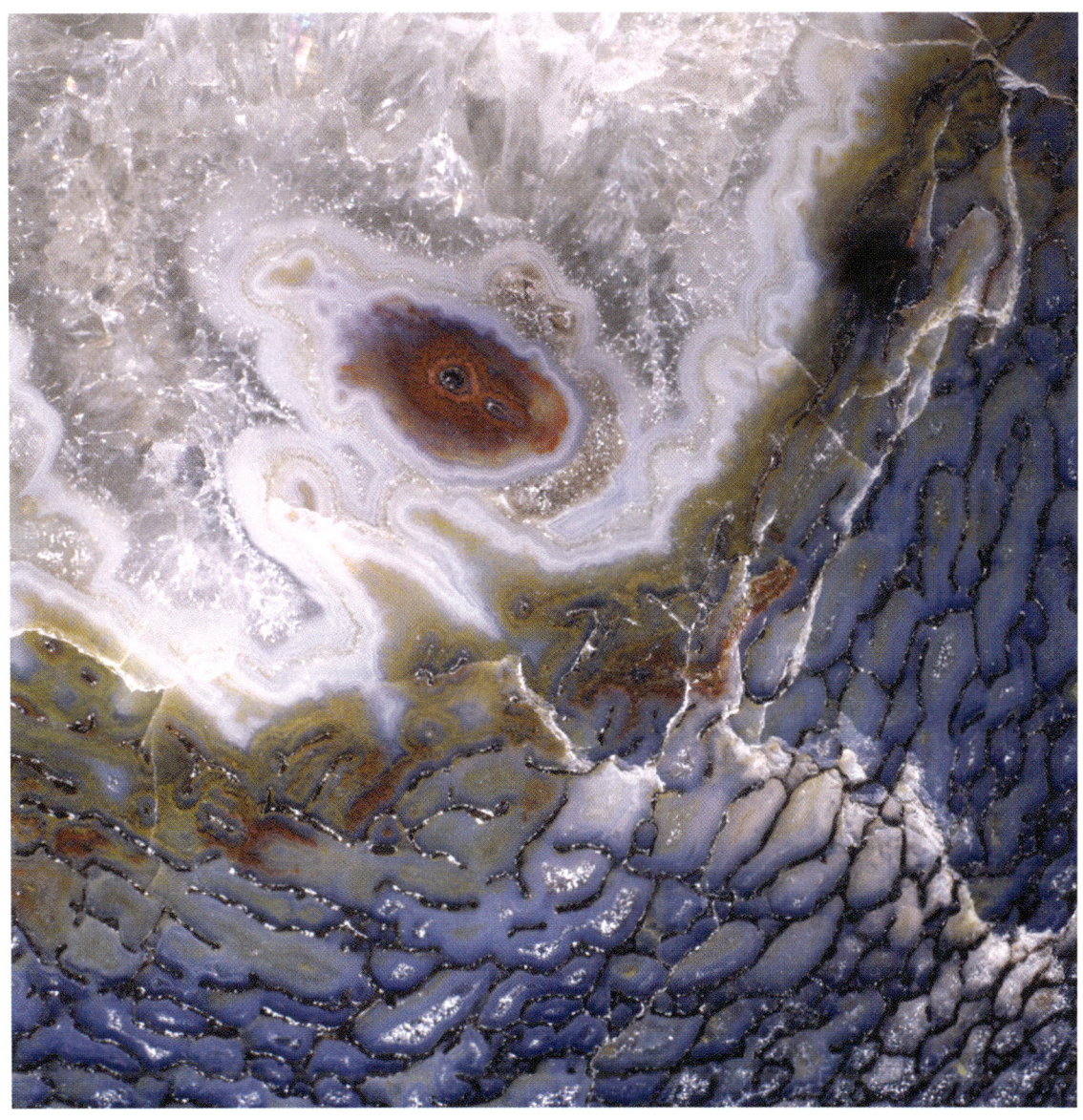

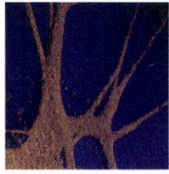

Chris J. Barry

Iris Anomaly, 2007

Slit lamp photograph; photo-slit lamp camera equipped with adjustable external electronic flash lighting

Lions Eye Institute, Perth, Australia

This ophthalmic photograph reveals a rare, congenital, and incomplete iris formation that was present at birth. This condition is likely to lead to the development of glaucoma later in life as a direct consequence of the malformations of the iris and related structures. In this region of the eye there are a number of muscles and connective tissues that all work synchronously. The stroma found in the iris connects sphincter muscles which contracts the pupil, and a set of dilator muscles that allow the iris to open. The back surface of the iris is covered by a pigmented epithelial layer, and the front of the iris has no epithelium. The high pigment content blocks light from passing through the iris. The iris influences the effects on intraocular pressure and indirectly on vision. The ability to see the physiology of this condition is greatly aided by using the photo-slit lamp camera. The very small and highly directional light produced by this instrument allows visualization of structural details often invisible using other more common illumination techniques.

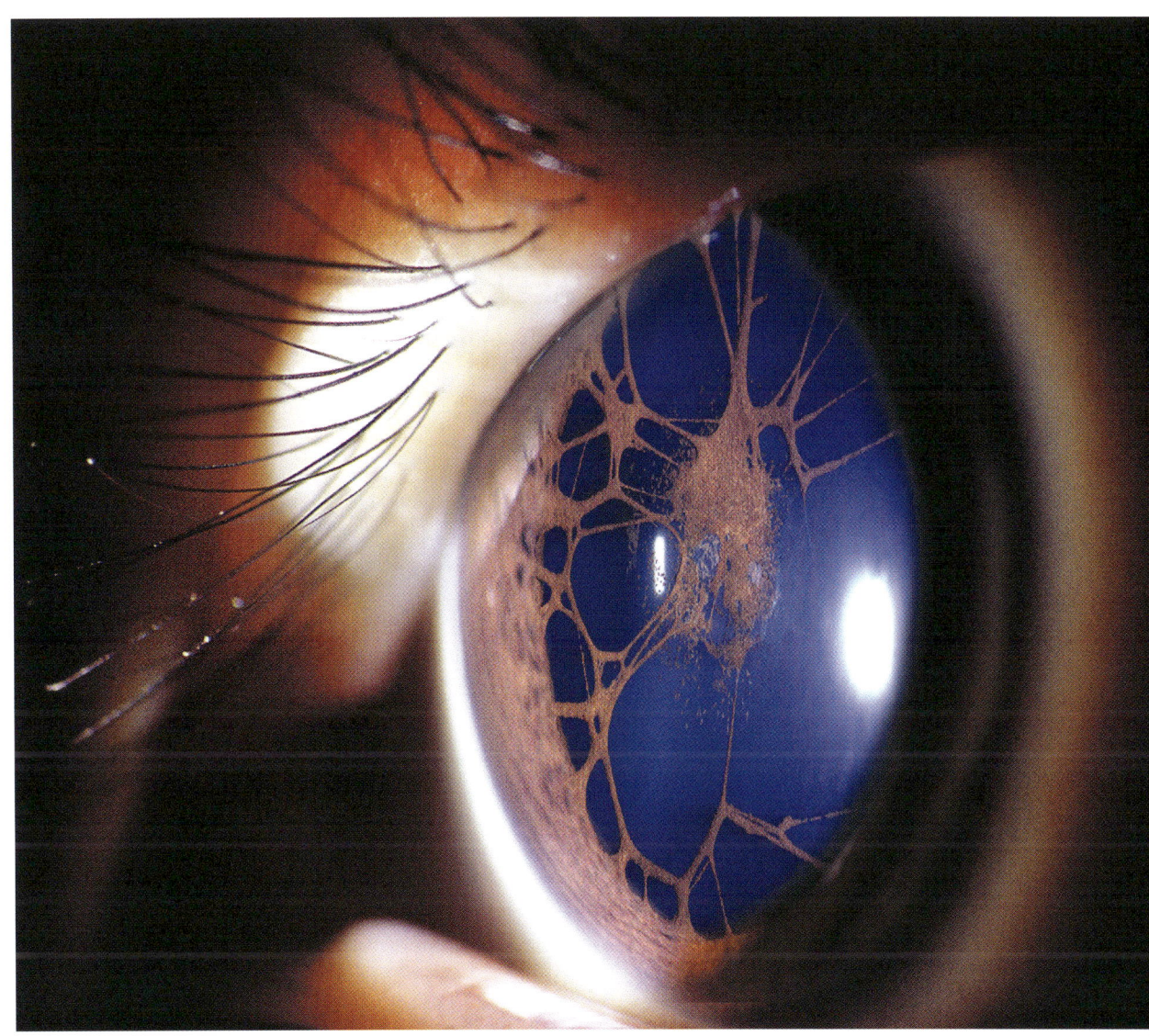

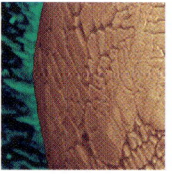

Dee Breger

Carpentaria Impact Spherule, 2007

Scanning electron photomicrograph; magnification approximately ×70 at capture; post-capture digital colorization

Drexel University, Department of Materials Science and Engineering, Philadelphia, Pennsylvania, United States

The magnetite (iron oxide) microspherule visible in this photomicrograph provides evidence of twin comet impacts into northern Australia's Gulf of Carpentaria in the year 536 CE. This evidence is part of a controversial study indicating that there has been a higher rate of cosmic impacts since the last ice age than have been documented and that some have changed the course of human history. This little fragment was melted or vaporized and flung into the atmosphere during the impact, crackling in a "quench texture" from rapid cooling as it condensed and fell back to Earth. The 536 CE impacts contributed to severe global cooling for the next 18 months that led to famines, wars, major population migrations, the first emergence of the Bubonic Plague, and the beginning of the Dark Ages.

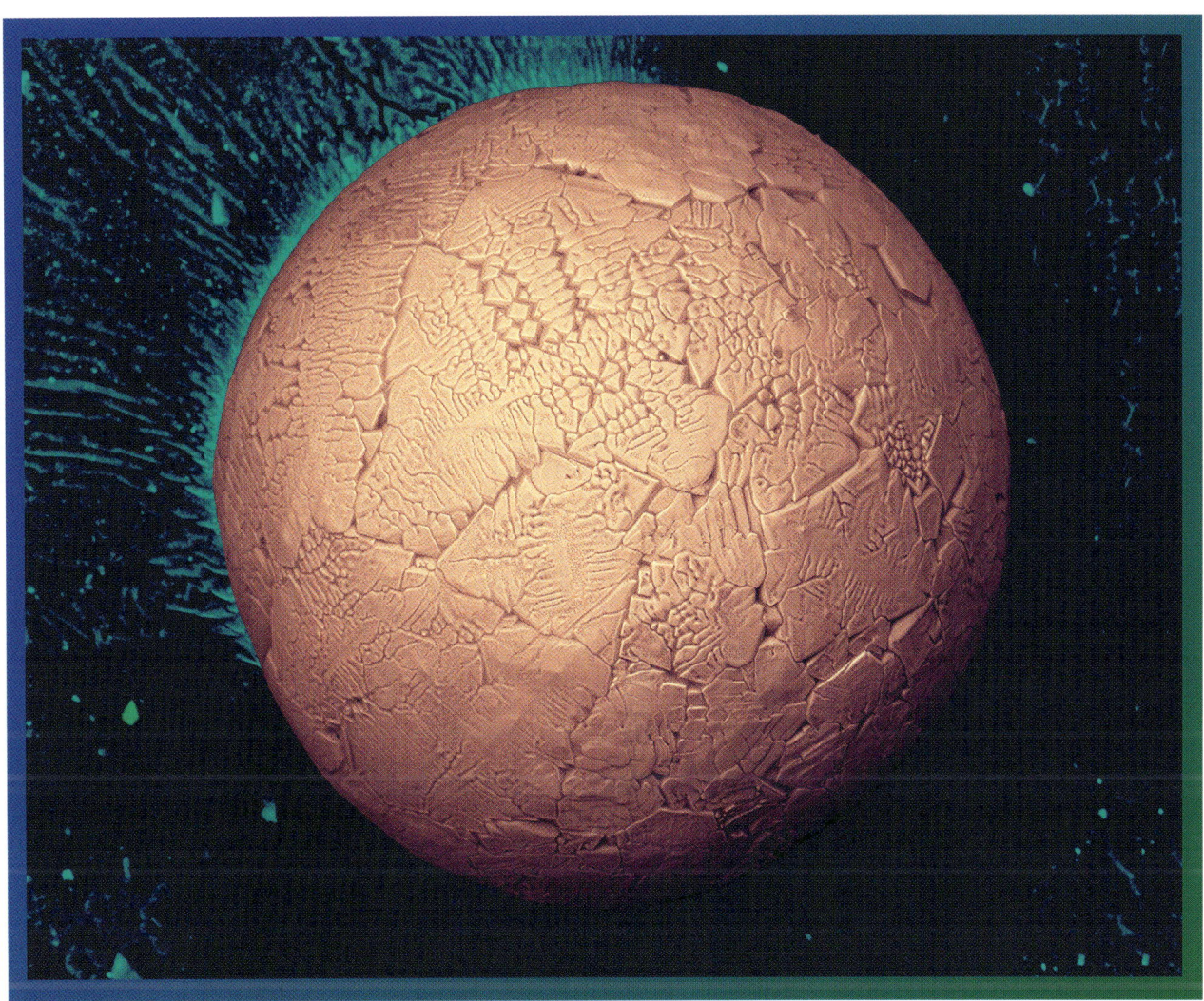

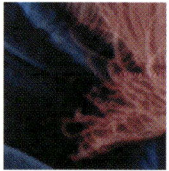

Kevin Brennan and Will Jaeckle

Feed Me: The Corona of *Brachionus plicatilis*, 2005

Scanning electron photomicrograph; magnification approximately ×800 at capture; post-capture digital colorization in 2008

Illinois Wesleyan University, Biology Department, Bloomington, Illinois, United States

Rotifers are small, water-dwelling animals that are an important food source for larval fish and crustaceans. Their name is derived from the Latin word for "wheel-bearer," and refers to the crown or corona of cilia, or hair-like projections around their mouths. This ventral view of an adult rotifer, *Brachionus plicatilis,* photographed using a scanning electron microscope, reveals the coronal ciliature and the break in the ciliature, which allows for delivery of particulate foods into an organism's mouth. When viewing the animal head on, the post-oral ciliature will beat in a clockwise metachronal or synchronized wave to draw the food into the mouth.

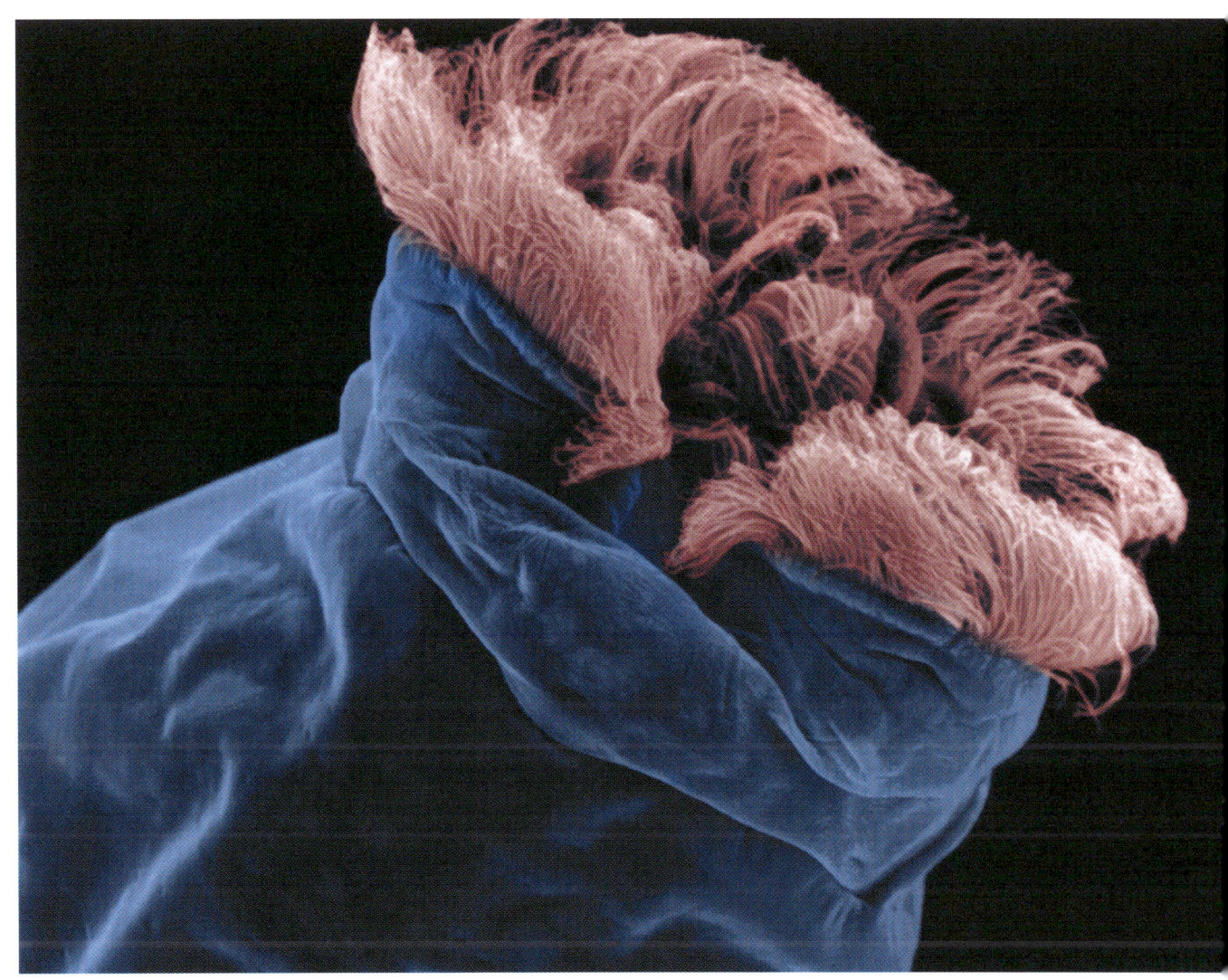

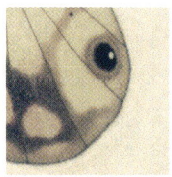

Linda L. Broadfoot

Cithaerias pyropina, Pyropine Ghost Satyr, 2002

Photomacrograph; 20 × 24 Polaroid camera; original photographic process used Polaroid image transfer onto Fabriano paper (receiver) and was produced at the Polaroid Studio, NYC January 24, 2002

Atlantic Beach, Florida, United States

While investigating some of nature's wonders as new subjects for my artwork, several butterfly specimens were borrowed from the Museum of Entomology, Florida State Collection of Arthropods, in Gainesville, Florida. These were photographed using the 20 × 24 Polaroid camera in New York, one of five such cameras in the world using simple flat lighting to reveal color and structure. To create this image an initial camera exposure was made using the 5-foot-tall, 235-pound view camera and then the dyes from the Polaroid film receptor sheet were pressed into a large dampened sheet of watercolor paper. Rubbing and pushing the transferred dyes by hand refined the final photograph's appearance, which was desired to evoke the sense of a natural history document. This work is one of a series of over 60 images produced over the course of five years, culminating in an artists' book, *INSECTA*.

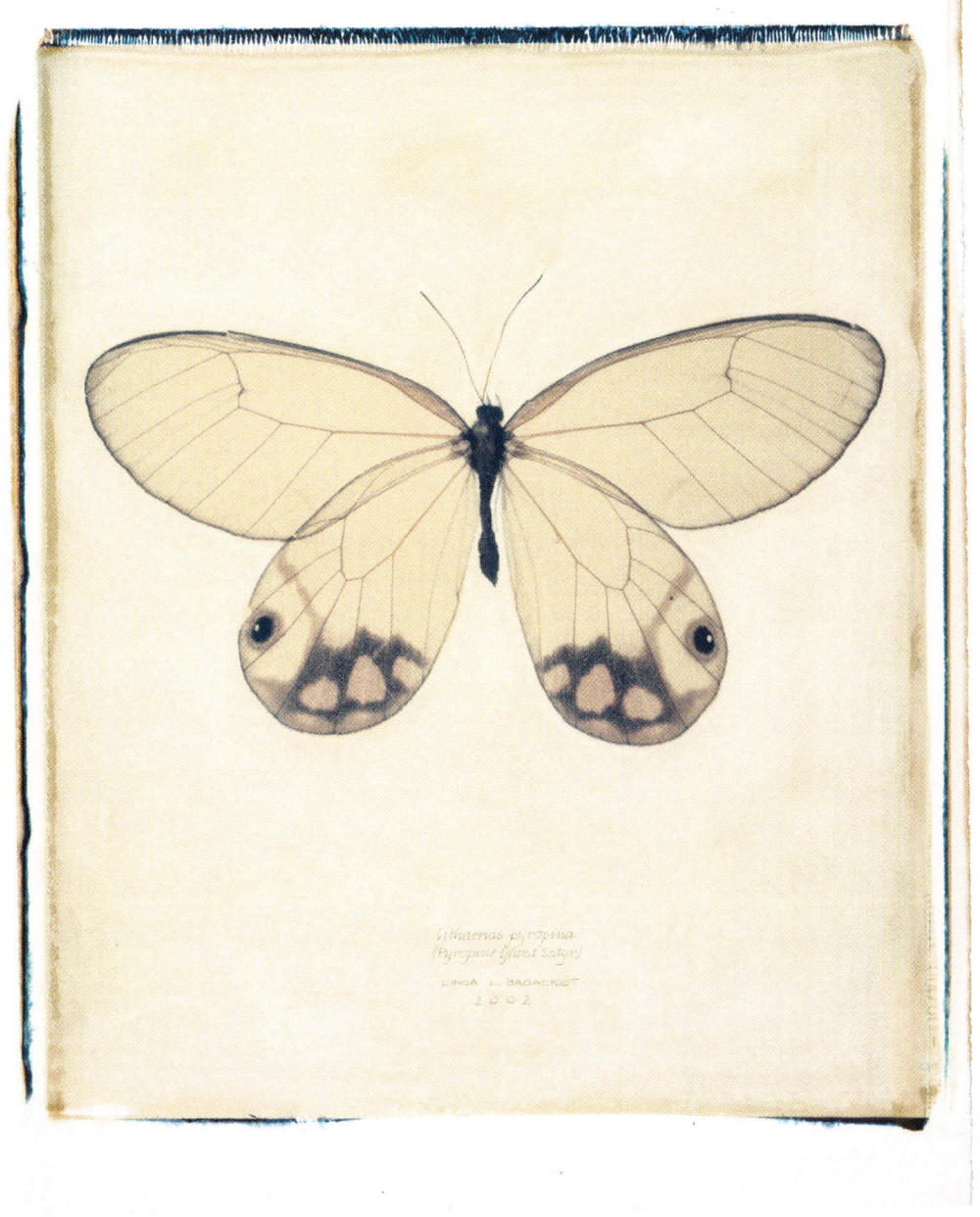

Lithaerias pyropasia
(Pyropura) (Glass Satyr)

LINDA L. BROADFOOT
2 0 0 2

13

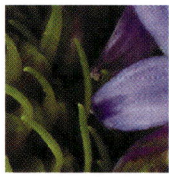

Thom Brommerich

Carribean Lily, *Scilla peruviana*, 2005

Photomacrograph; direct digital capture

Thom-B-Foto, Orangevale, California, United States

This photograph reveals the structures of the Caribbean Lily, or *Scilla peruviana*, a bulb-bearing herbaceous perennial plant, which is ironically misnamed. It is not from the Caribbean or Peru but rather, this plant is native to the Mediterranean area. *Scilla peruviana* is a bulb-bearing perennial plant. The bloom consists of 50–100 tiny flowers with 6 petals. Colors range from white to blue to purple. This image made using available light and a digital camera with a macro lens reveals the entire flower, which was 1–2 cm in diameter and reveals the tiny flowers and petals.

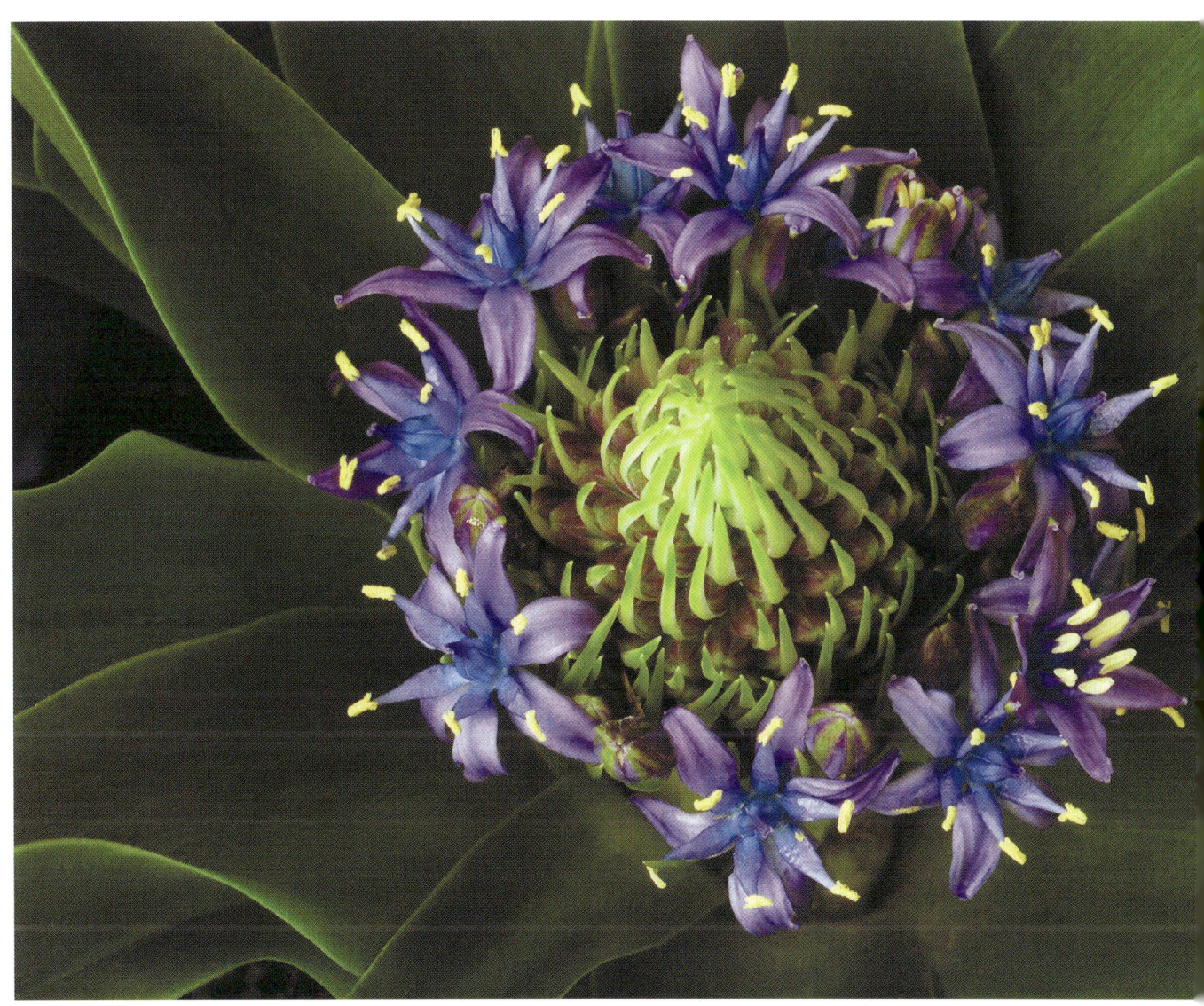

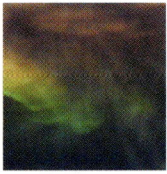

Thom Brommerich

Circumhorizontal Arc, 2005

Natural science photograph; direct digital capture

Thom-B-Foto, Orangevale, California, United States

A circumhorizontal arc is a rare optical weather phenomenon that appears as a horizontal rainbow. It is caused by the refraction of light through ice crystals in cirrus clouds, which only occurs when the sun is high and at least 58° above the horizon. The ice crystals must be aligned horizontally to refract the sun presenting this unusual pattern. When light rays enter the hexagonal crystals in a vertical orientation, they will exit through the horizontal bottom face causing the light rays to refract or bend. An example of this happens when light passes through a prism. The 90° refraction of the light produces the stacked rainbow effect, which is also known as a flaming or fire rainbow.

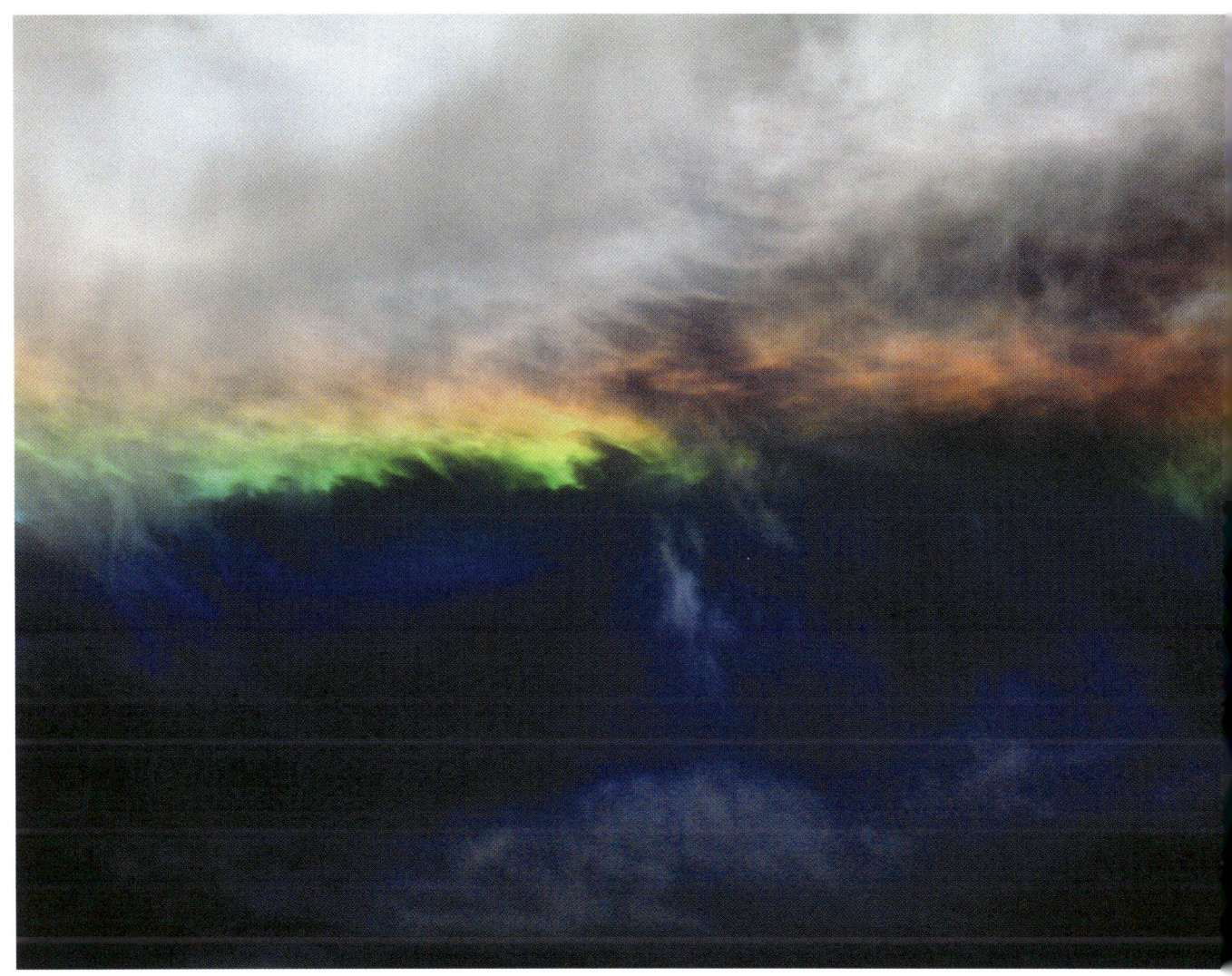

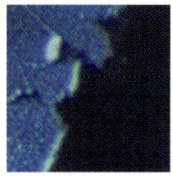

Angela Chappell

Pseudoexfoliation of Human Eye, 2001

Slit lamp photograph, color transparency film

Ophthalmology Department, Flinders Medical Centre, Bedford Park, Australia

Pseudoexfoliation includes fibrillar deposits, which appear like flakes in the anterior chamber of the eye on the ocular lens capsule. Pseudoexfoliation is a disease that occurs in the aging of the lens capsule and is a major risk factor for the development of a type of glaucoma that can progress to blindness. Because this condition is located in the anterior chamber of the eye in a region almost invisible to human vision, specialized lighting from a slit lamp is required to make it visible. In this type of work, the tiniest of structures are made visible using a narrow and highly angular lighting.

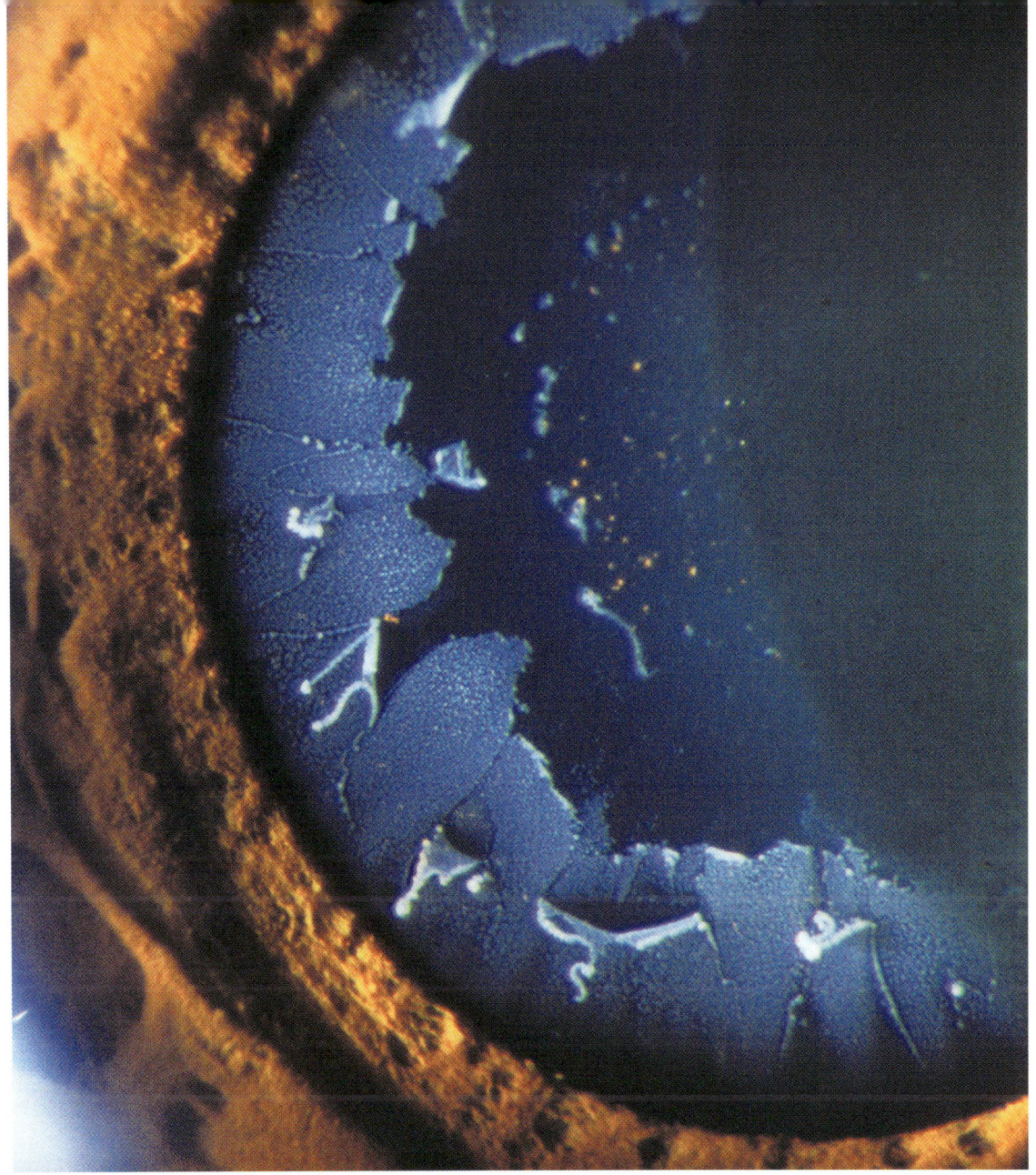

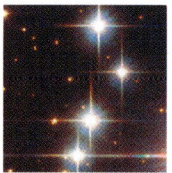

Lars Christensen

Star on a Hubble Diet

Astrophotograph; Wide Field and Planetary Camera 2 and the
Advanced Camera for Surveys on board the Hubble Space Telescope

Space Telescope European Coordinating Facility, European Space Agency/Hubble &
NASA, Munich, Germany

The star cluster Pismis 24 lies in the core of the large emission nebula NGC 6357
that extends one degree on the sky in the direction of the Scorpius constellation.
A region in the nebula has been ionized over time by the youngest (bluest) heavy
stars in Pismis 24. The intense ultraviolet radiation from the blazing stars heats the
gas surrounding the cluster and creates a bubble in NGC 6357. The presence of the
surrounding gas clouds makes probing into the region difficult.

This image is a composite of many separate exposures made by the ACS and WFPC2
instruments on the Hubble Space Telescope using several different filters. Five filters
were used to sample both broad and narrow wavelength ranges. The color picture
results from assigning different colors to each of the monochromatic images. Image
credits: NASA, ESA and Jesús Maíz Apellániz—Instituto de astrofísica de Andalucía,
Spain and acknowledgements to Davide De Martin—ESA/Hubble.

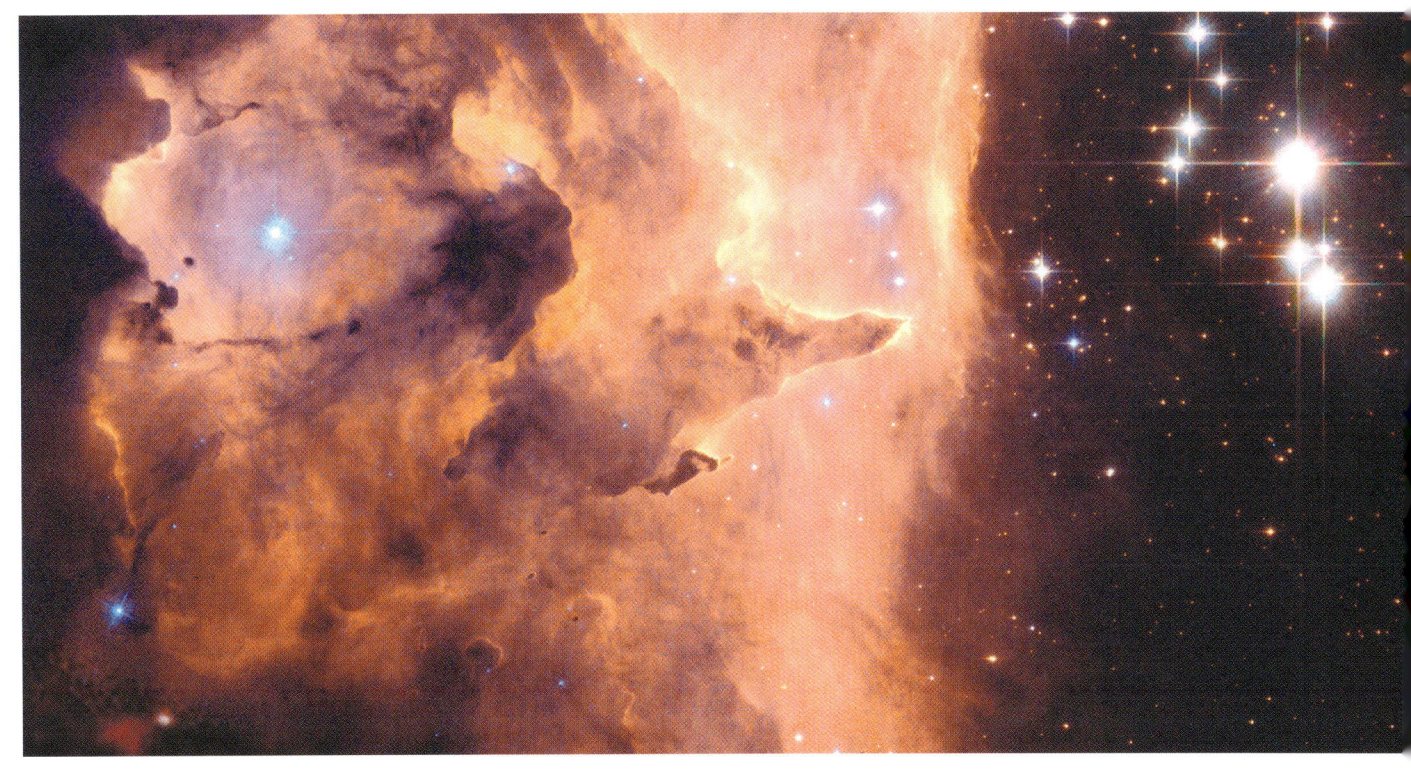

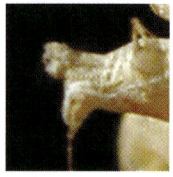

George Cook

Crane Fly Larva, Posterior View, 2002

Photomicrograph; compound microscope; magnification approximately ×200 at capture; Nikon CoolPix 990 camera

Rochester, New York, United States

The presence of aquatic organisms in water can be used as a determination of water quality. For this to be the case, the found organisms must first be identified. Insect larvae are identified by studying their body parts at magnifications up to ~500×. Crane fly larvae are quite large and seldom require greater than 40×, observable in a high quality stereomicroscope.

Crane flies are in the insect order *Diptera* and family *Tipulidae*. More than 1,500 species of such flies have been described in North America alone. Their life cycle includes metamorphoses in stages from eggs, larvae, pupae, and the adult flying and breeding phase. A typical crane fly larvae is grub-like and lives in a variety of habitats including fresh water streams, muddy soils with decaying plant material, and some-times relatively dry soil such as those found in lawns. This photograph of the posterior of a crane fly larva is helpful in taxonomy for species identification. The arrangement of spiracles, or airways, surrounded by a ring of fleshy lobes varies from species to species, and easily visible in this magnification.

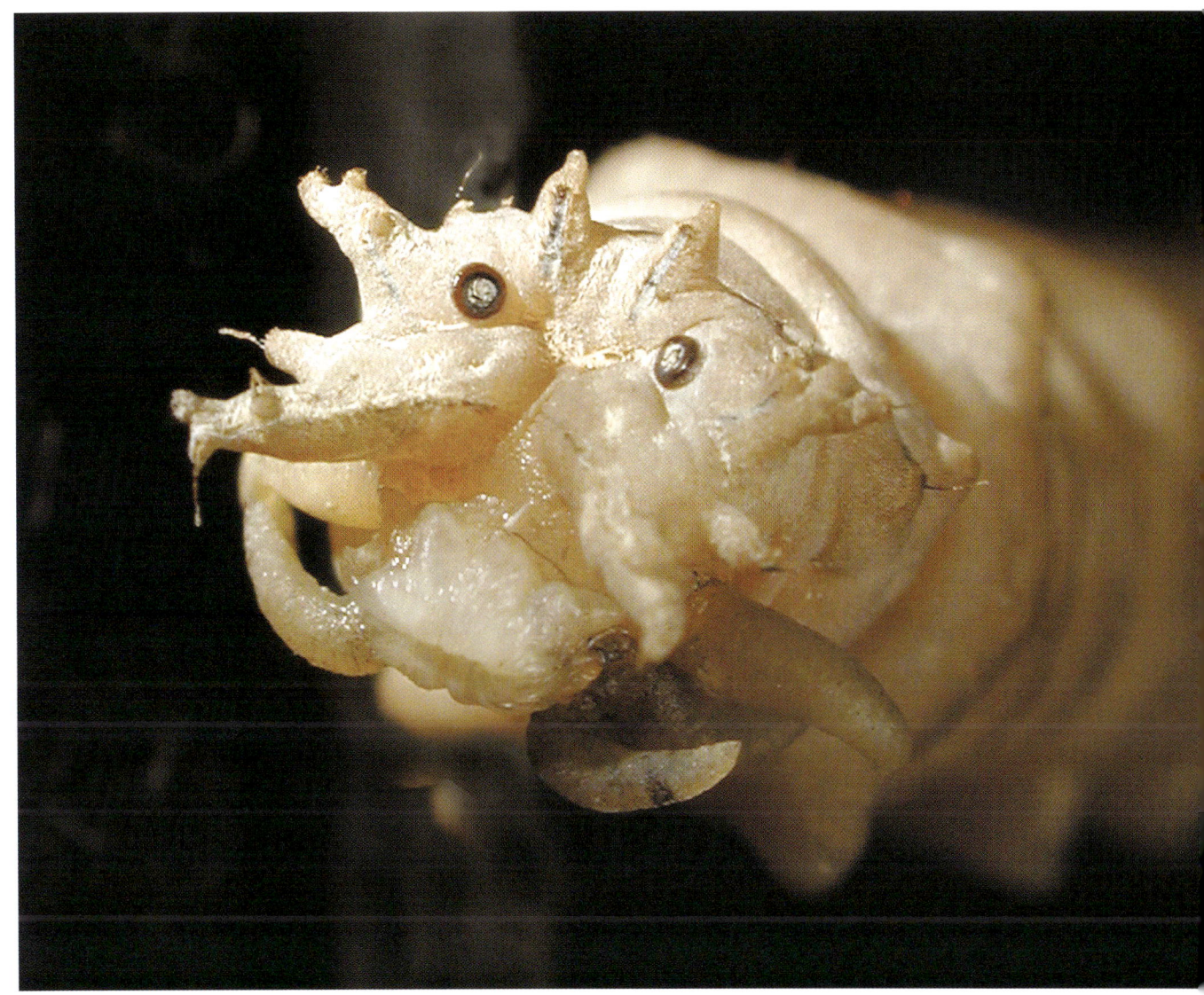

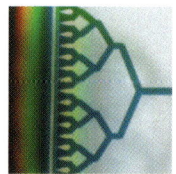

Gregory A. Cooksey

Microfluidics to Dye For, 2006

Photomacrograph; Canon 20D with 50mm F1.8 lens equipped with an EF25II extension tube; Canon 480EX flash and custom foil reflectors

National Institute for Standards and Technology (NIST), Gaithersburg, Virginia, United States

This image documents a microfluidic network that was filled with food coloring to increase visibility of the channels, which are 200 micrometers in diameter and lead to a central chamber of approximately 4 × 6 mm. This device was designed to select combinations of 16 unique chemicals (represented by the different colored dyes) for delivery into the central reaction chamber. Actuation of the pneumatic channels that have open and close valves route fluids through the device which are made of polydimethylsiloxane (PDMS), a transparent, flexible polymer. The small dimensions of the network created laminar flow patterns (as observed in the central chamber), whereby adjacent flow streams mixed only by diffusion (slowly, over long distances). A number of features in the device make it well suited for a multitude of chemical and biological experiments. This research was undertaken at the University of Washington, Department of Bioengineering.

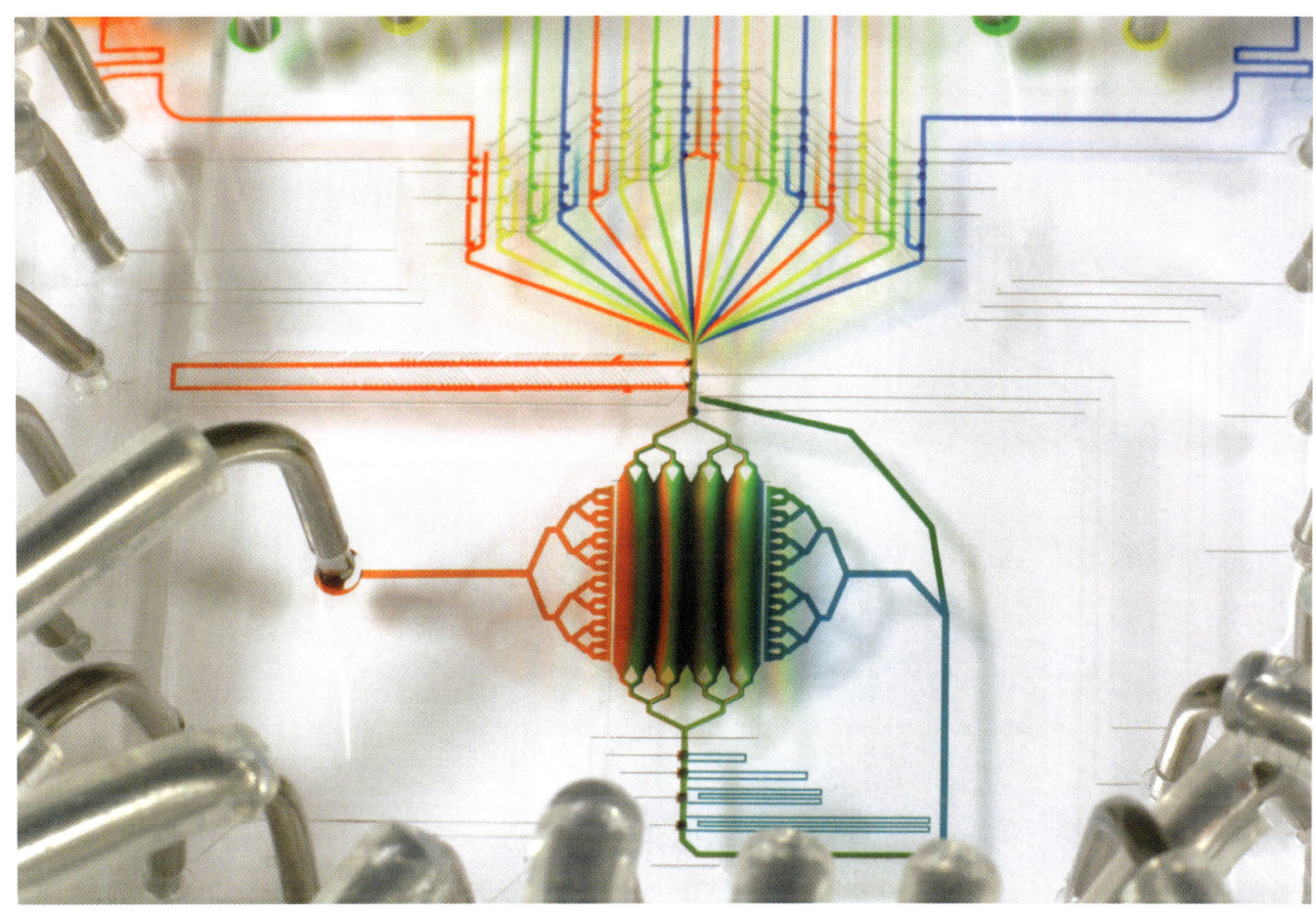

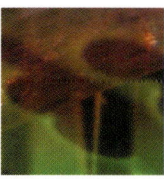

Gregory A. Cooksey

Material Mood, 2006

Photomacrograph; Canon 20D camera with 50 mm F1.8 lens and equipped with a EF25II extension tube; polarizing filters; exposed using sunlight

National Institute for Standards and Technology (NIST), Gaithersburg, Virginia, United States

Stainless steel needles inserted into a microfluidic device are visible in this photograph. Because of its size and application, it was placed in a petri dish to take the photograph. This image is the result of a series of images that recorded the birefringence or double refraction of the polystyrene dish, which produces brilliant colors throughout the transparent microfluidic device. This research was carried out at the University of Washington, Department of Bioengineering.

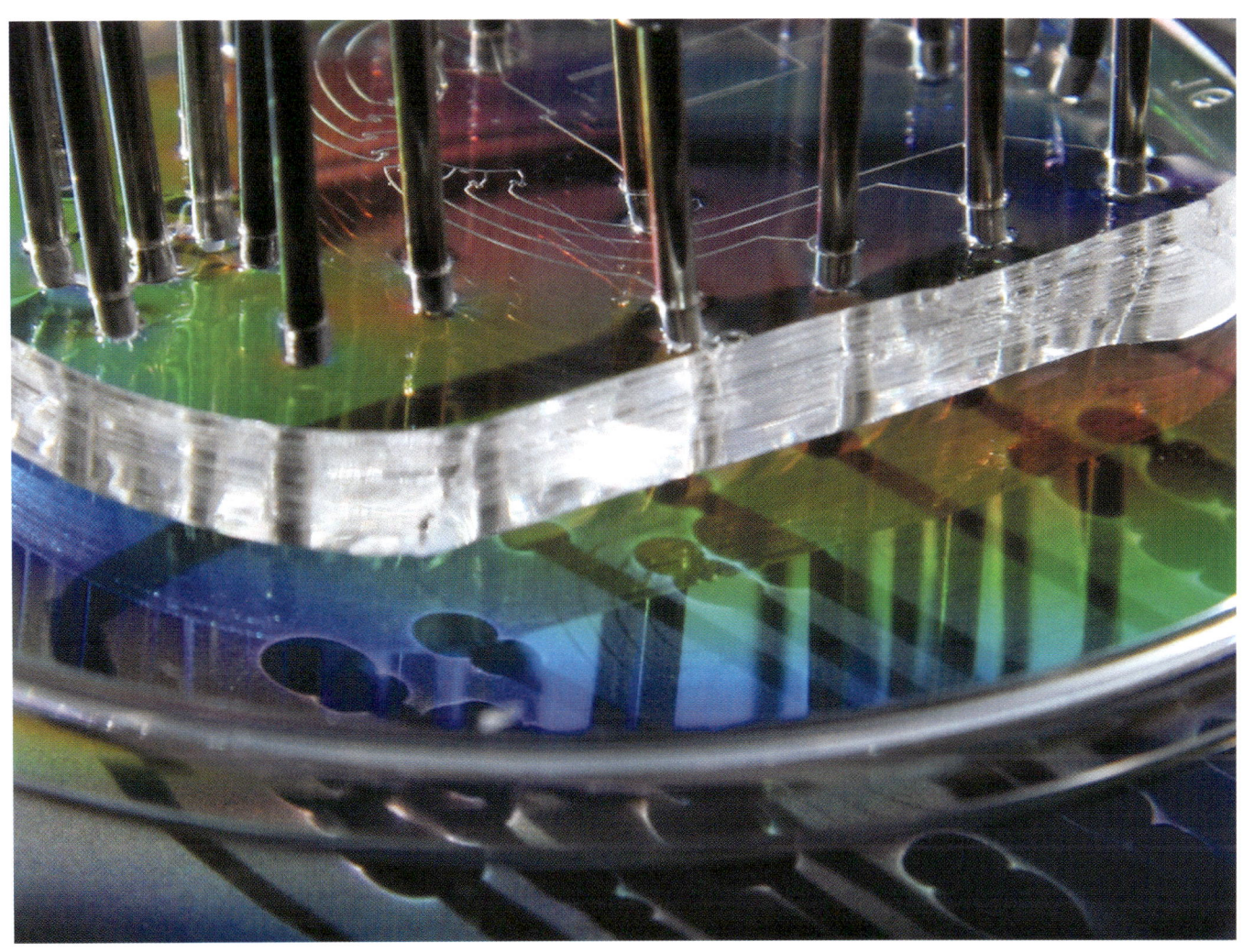

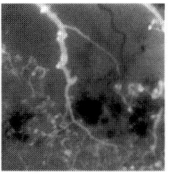

Paul Crompton

Superotemporal Retinal Branch Vein Occlusion, 2001

Fundus photograph; Topcon 50IX fundus camera; Kodak Megaplus digital monochromatic camera

Media Resources Centre, Cardiff & Vale NHS Trust and Cardiff University,
University Hospital of Wales, Cardiff, United Kingdom

Fluorescein angiography of the fundus is a technique in which a small amount of sodium fluorescein dye is injected in to the arm of the patient and then photographed as it passes through the blood vessels of the retina, using a short wave blue light to excite the dye. A sequence of photographs is taken as the dye travels through the circulatory system, passing from arteries to veins. The contrast achieved by using the dye allows the ophthalmologist to clearly see problems with the blood flow to this vital organ.

In this image, one of the veins taking blood away from the upper half of the retina reveals it is blocked. The blood (and dye) entering through the fully functioning arterial system cannot pass through the capillary network to the vein in the normal way and so tries to find alternative routes by crossing to the circulation in the lower half of the eye. Meanwhile, the capillary system in the affected area is shut down, illustrated by the marked difference between the general appearances of the two halves of the retina.

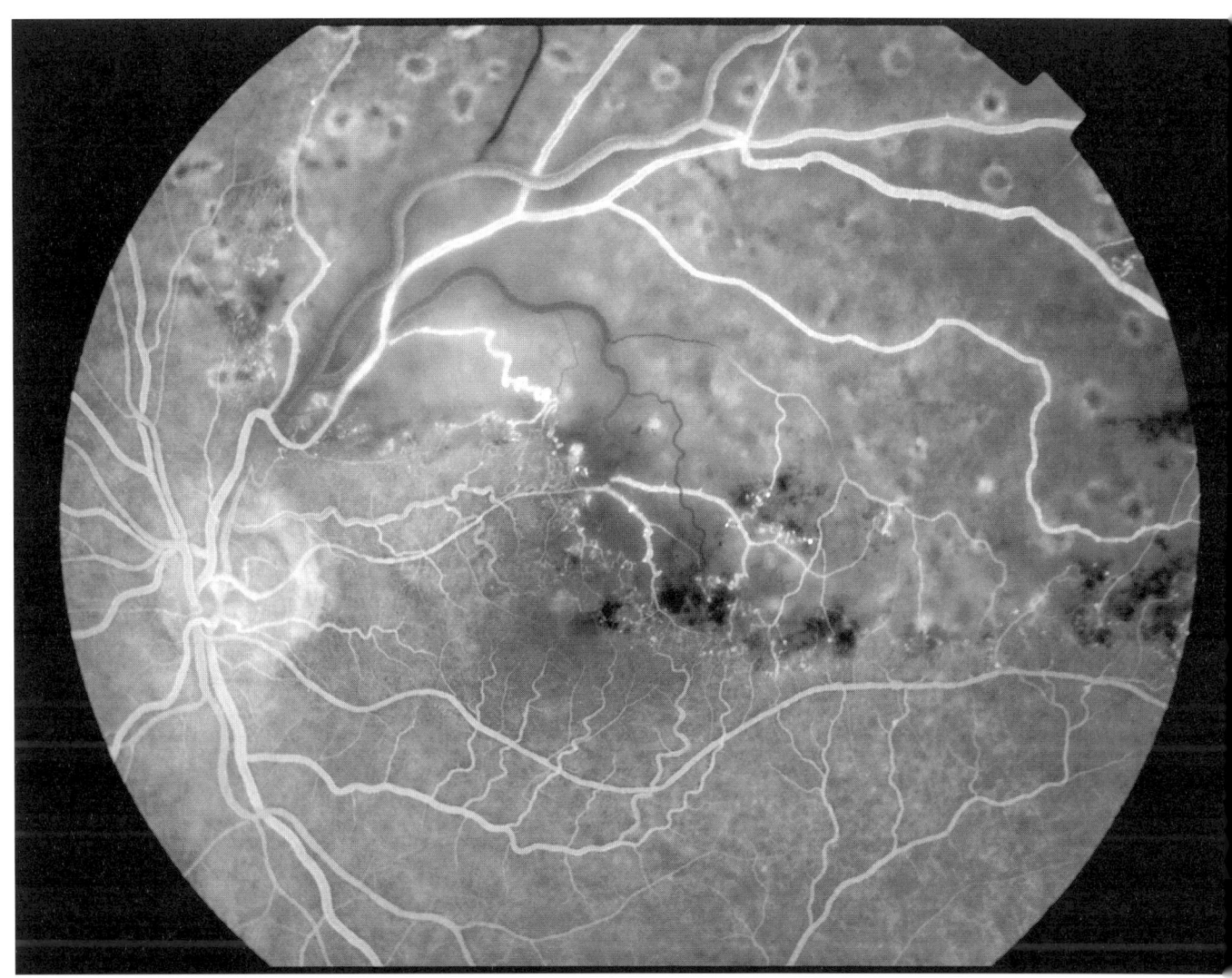

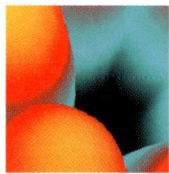

Hans U. Danzebrink

Aesthetic Imperfections, 2008

Atomic force photomicrograph; magnification approximately ×350,000 at capture; sample approximately 1.5 μm × 2.5 μm in size; post-capture colorization

Physikalisch-Technische Bundesanstalt (PTB), Braunschweig, Germany

This image reveals dislocations in a photonic crystal arrangement of polystyrene nanospheres magnified from a sample size of about 1.5 μm × 2.5 μm. In this case, the photonic crystals were grown as self-assembled structures from a colloidal solution. The nanospheres measure about 200 nm in diameter and are about 300 times smaller than a human hair, but still approximately 500 times larger than atoms. Practically, photonic crystals can be used to control and manipulate the flow of light, e.g. in optical waveguides. Even in nature, this type of nanosphere arrangement can be found. A classic example of this is observed in the gemstone opal with its iridescent play of light colors. Thorsten Dziomba of PTB provided the image data, and Dr. Frank Marlow of Max-Planck-Institut für Kohlenforschung supplied the sample. WSxM software was used to carry out the post-capture colorization.

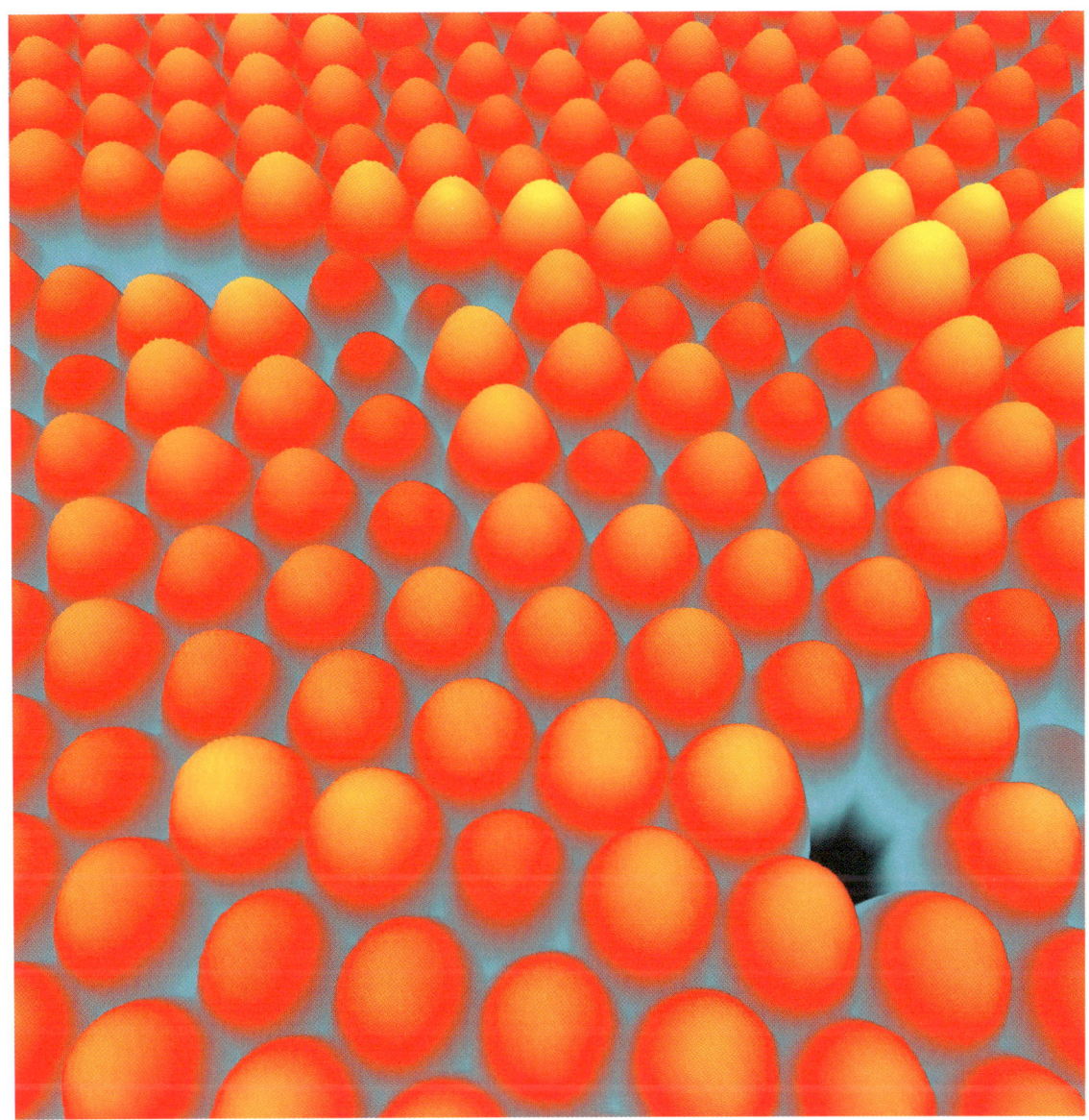

31

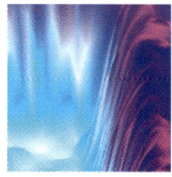

Hans U. Danzebrink and Anna-Maria Gleixner

Data Channels, 2007

Atomic force photomicrograph; magnification approximately ×35,000 at capture; actual sample approximately 15 μm × 25 μm in size; post-capture colorization

Physikalisch-Technische Bundesanstalt (PTB), Braunschweig, Germany

This circuit-level image of a computer chip is a magnified view from a sample, which measures approximately 15 μm × 25 μm. The blue water-like coloring symbolizes the flow of information inside the microprocessor. The image data was provided by the nanometrologist Thorsten Dziomba, also of PTB, and the post-capture colorization was performed using WSxM scanning probe microscopy software for data visualization.

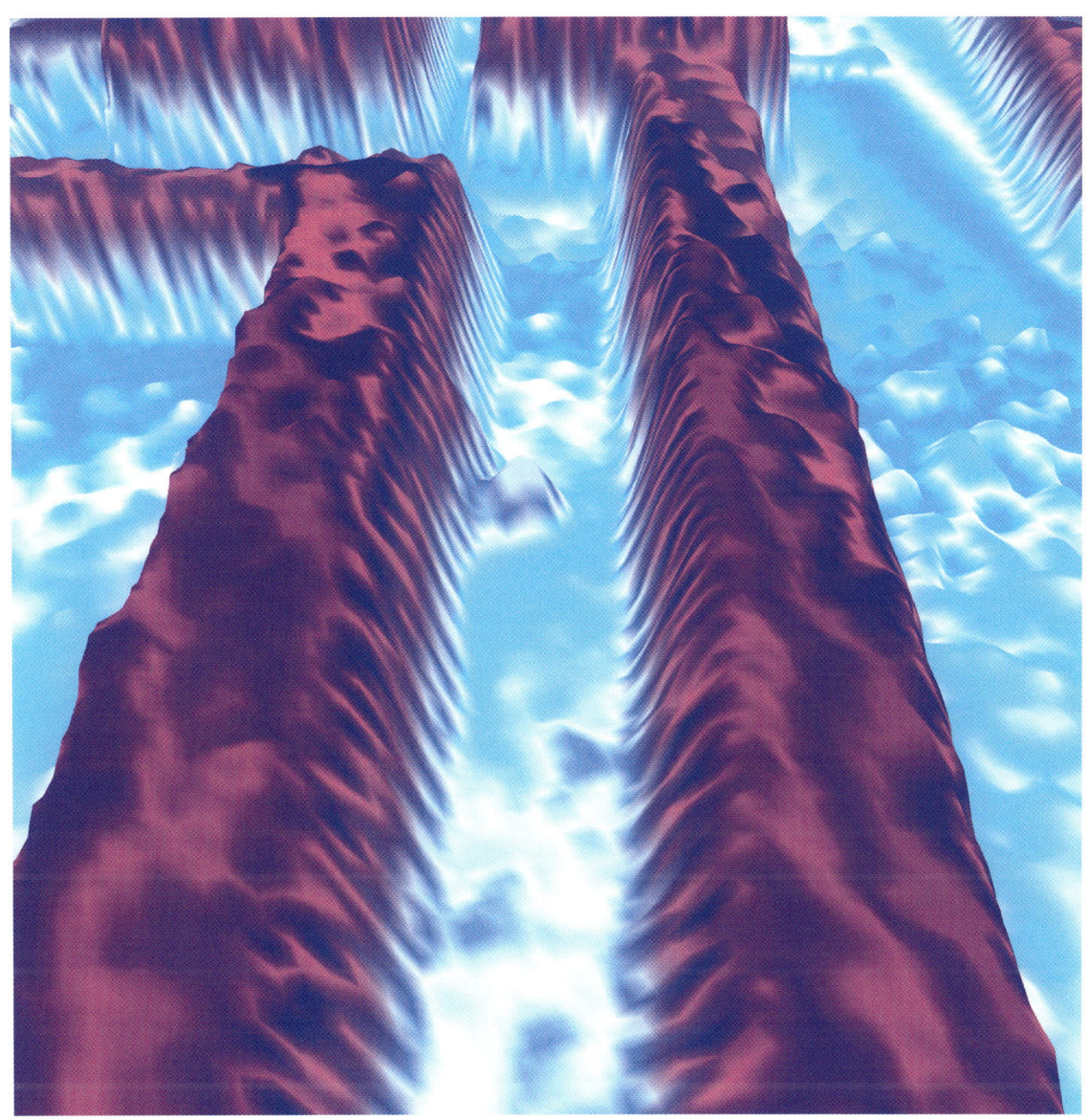

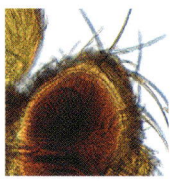

José Estévez

Fly Away, April 2000

Photomacrograph; color transparency film

Mayaguez, Puerto Rico

The fruit fly, *Drosophila melanogaster,* is approximately 3 mm in length and is one of the most significant organisms in biological research, particularly in genetics and developmental biology. It has helped humans better understand the principles of genetics and inheritance. The *Drosophila* specimen was prepared as a microscope slide by Wards' Natural Science Est. Inc. and photographed in the Biomedical Photographic Communications Laboratories at the Rochester Institute of Technology.

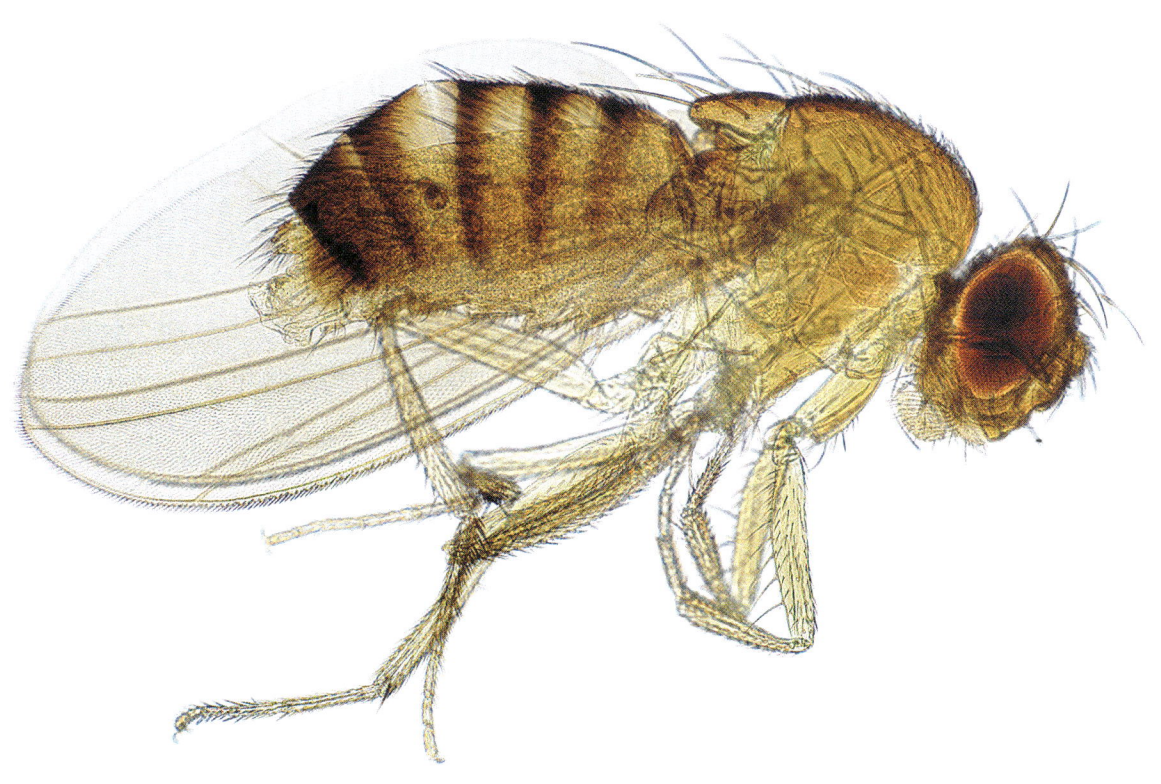

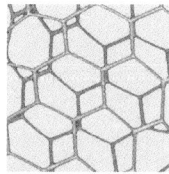

Felice Frankel

Nanotubes, 2008

Scientific Illustration; flatbed scan of enlarged film image

Harvard University, Initiative in Innovative Computing, Cambridge, Massachusetts, United States

This image is a representation of carbon nanotubes. Although not an image of actual nanotubules, it has provided insightful and valuable information used to describe the physical structure and organization of nanotubes. This image was created by the manipulation of an image produced from a flatbed scanner. Initially, a black hexagonal pattern representing a standard carbon lattice was printed on an 8 × 10 inch piece of transparent acetate which was rolled into a tube and oriented in a way that the object would be organized. This film tube was then scanned using the flatbed scanner at a very high resolution and tonal scale.

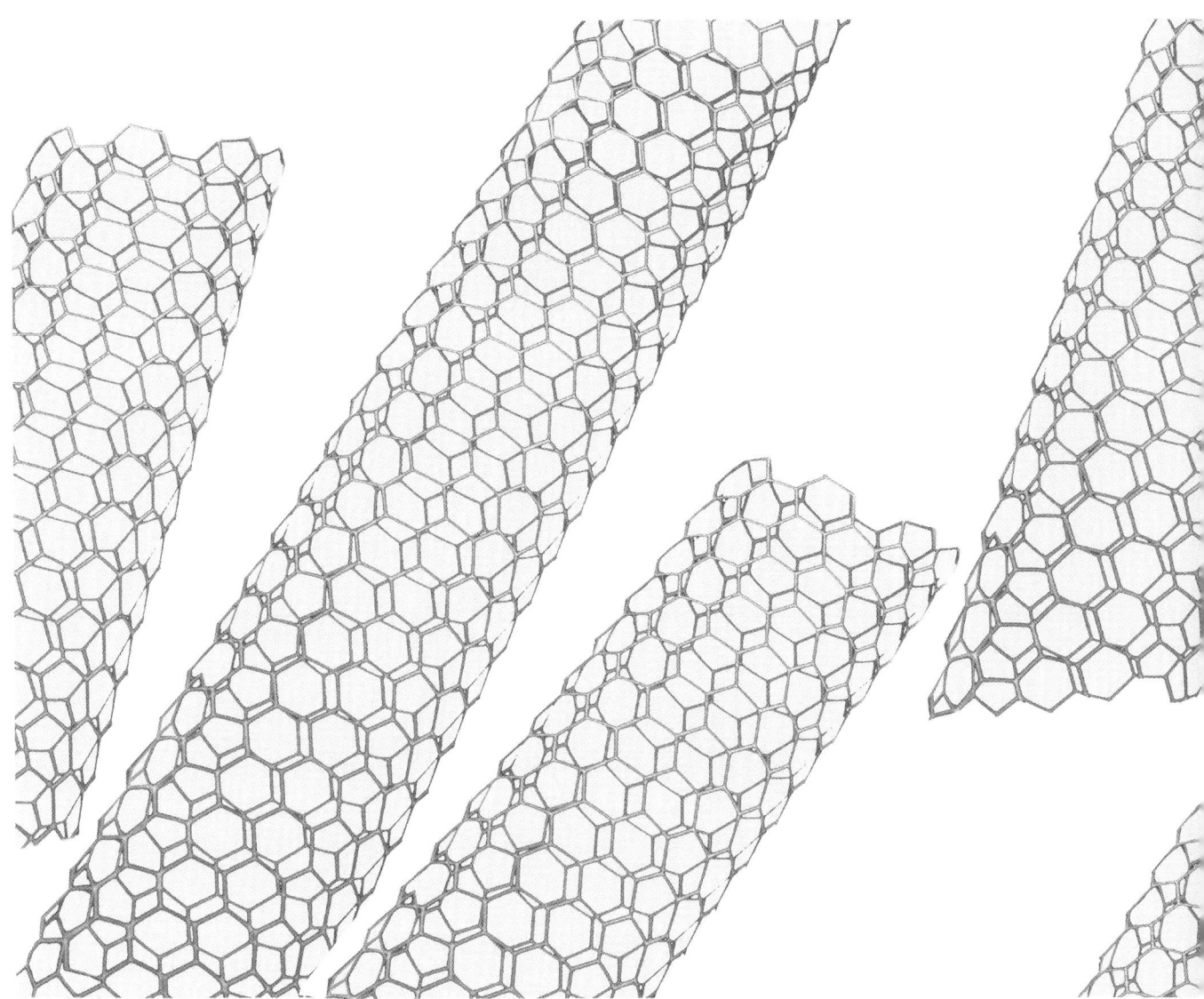

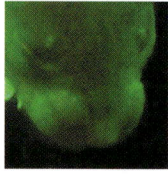

James E. Hayden

GFP Mouse and Offspring, 2003

Fluorescence photograph; Nikon CoolPix 990 digital camera; Illumatool LT-9900 light source with excitation at 470nm and a 515nm barrier filter; additional ambient light—tungsten source

The Wistar Institute, Philadelphia, Pennsylvania, United States

Green Fluorescent Protein (GFP) has become an important part of biological investigations that requires non-invasive labeling of cells, especially in vivo. Derived from the jellyfish *Aequorea victoria*, GFP can be integrated directly into the DNA of a cell where it will naturally emit green fluorescence when excited with the proper blue wavelength. The fluorescence that is produced can then be used as a marker to follow a variety of biological events, from aging and cancer development to protein synthesis and xenotransplantation.

Researchers initially injected GFP-tagged spermatogonial stem cells into recipient male mice to see if the introduced cells would be viable for sperm production. All of the cells in mice produced from these stem cells then fluoresced, as shown by the adult mouse in the image (the emitted green light is blocked by hair, so only the parts of the mouse with little hair, like the tail, paws and ears, show green). With the GFP incorporated into its genome, the male mouse then passed the "green gene," through normal Mendelian genetics, to its offspring. The mouse pup that inherited the gene fluoresces like its father, while the remaining siblings, who did not receive the gene with the GFP, do not. This image is the result of a combination of two original digital images, taken seconds apart.

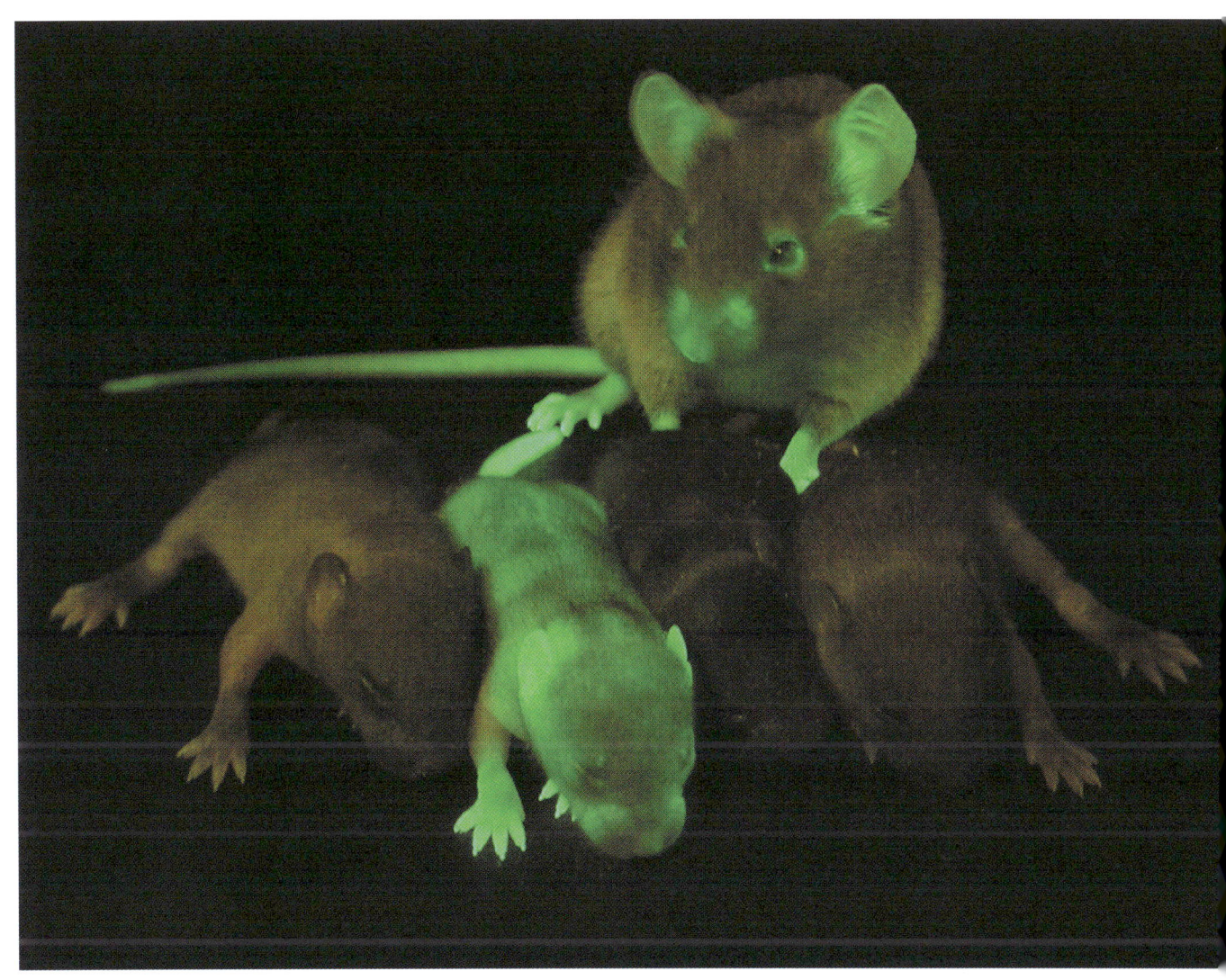

39

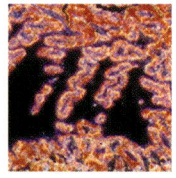

James E. Hayden

Iris, Ciliary Body and Lens in Canine Eye, 2000

Photomicrograph; magnification approximately ×7 at capture;
FXA Nikon photomicroscope; Kodak EPY transparency film

The Wistar Institute, Philadelphia, Pennsylvania, United States

Pathologists routinely examine sections cut from a variety of specimen types to help identify normal morphology as well as pathological conditions in diseased tissues. This section through a normal dog's eye was stained with hematoxylin and eosin as part of a common staining procedure, which demonstrates remarkable preservation of structures in the eye that are difficult to maintain as an intact sample. The overall composition has an uncanny resemblance to an aquatic bird. The "head" and "neck" of the bird make up part of the iris, the ciliary body (small muscles that pull the iris open) are seen as the "wing," and the lens appears as a large "moon" at the top left.

Visual enhancement of the image was achieved by using darkfield microscopy, which reverses the background from white to black and modifies the colors in the specimen. To complete the illusion, a small bit of blue color was introduced into the light path to add blue to the sclera, or "white" of the eye, creating the look of water along the bottom of the image.

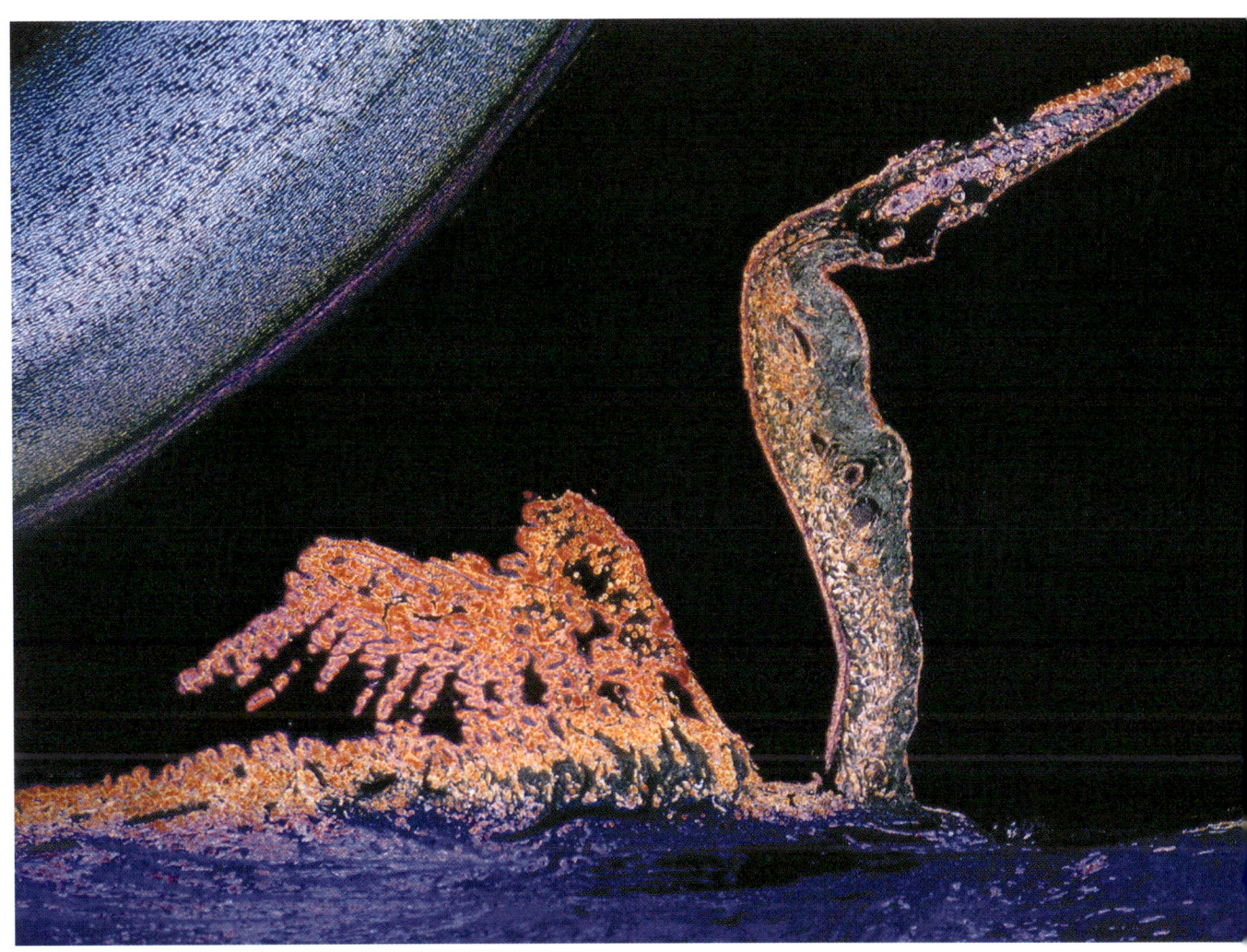

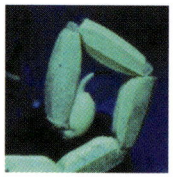

Bifurcation of the Tail and Ultraviolet Fluorescence in the Bark Scorpion *Centruroides exilicauda* (Buthidae), 1997

Natural science photograph; Nikon FM; 35mm Kodak Kodachrome 64 film; Norman 200B flash unit; Lepp Bracket; UV imaging filter

Arizona Research Laboratories, Division of Neurobiology, The University of Arizona, Tucson, Arizona, United States

This image of an adult female shows a two-tailed bark scorpion and was exposed using the fluorescence technique using ultraviolet excitation. Bifurcation of the tail is thought to be the result of incomplete twinning. Two-tailed scorpions usually die during the molting process, which is typical of all invertebrates as they grow and few survive to become adults. Scorpions are among the oldest forms of arachnids and have long been known to fluoresce under ultraviolet excitation, a property known as photoluminescence. The role of fluorescence in scorpions, if any, is unknown.

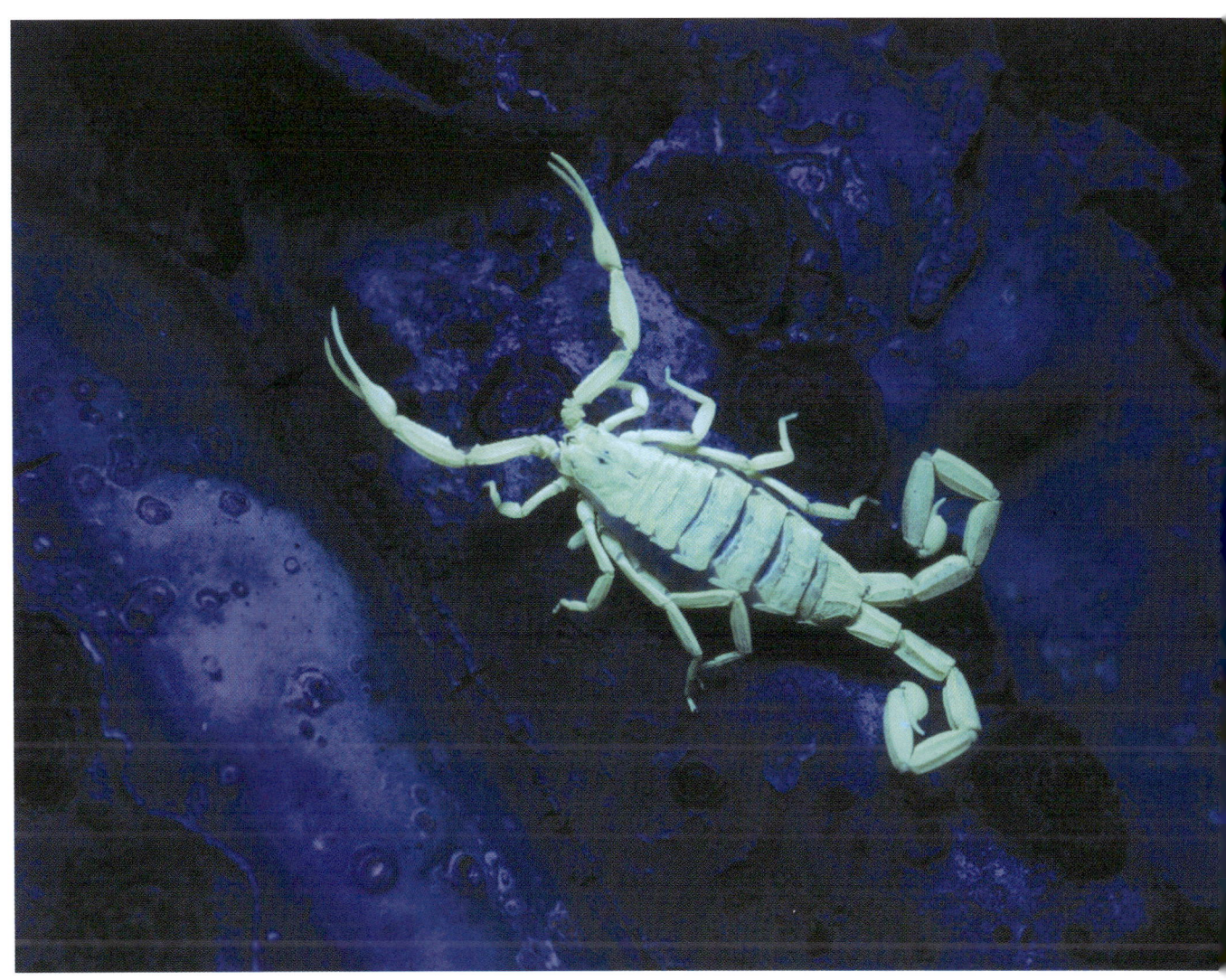

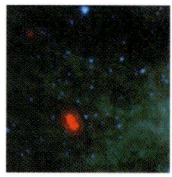

Robert L. Hurt

The Infrared Helix Nebula, 2007

Astrophotograph; Space Telescope; Infrared Array Camera (IRAC);
color assignments: 3.6 microns (blue), 4.5 microns (green),
5.8 microns (orange), 8.0 microns (red)

Spitzer Science Center, Pasadena, California, United States

This infrared image created from NASA's Spitzer Space Telescope shows the Helix Nebula, a cosmic starlet often photographed by amateur astronomers for its vivid colors and eerie resemblance to a giant eye. These peculiar clouds are the blown-off remains of a star that was once in the galaxy and believed to be similar to our own Sun. The blues and greens show the glow of a variety of elements expelled with the star's outer envelope, while the reds show longer wavelength infrared radiation emanating from dust particles closer to the inner stellar corpse, or white dwarf.

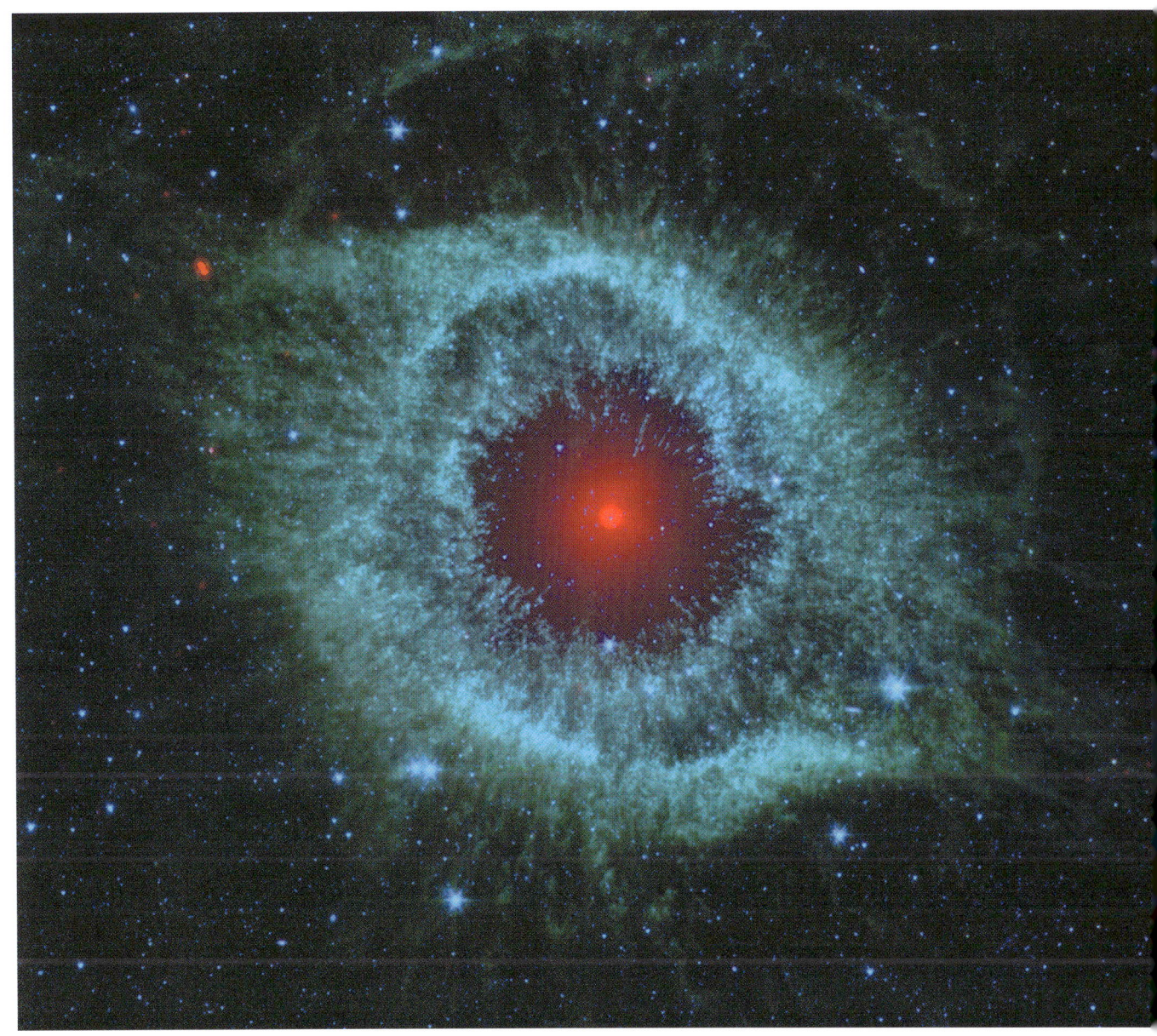

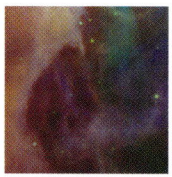

Robert L. Hurt

The (In)Visible Orion Nebula, 2006

Astrophotograph; Spitzer and Hubble Space Telescopes;
digital multi-wavelength capture and rendering

Spitzer Science Center, Pasadena, California, United States

NASA's Spitzer and Hubble Space Telescopes have often teamed up to expose the chaos that baby stars are creating 1,500 light-years away in the cosmic cloud called the Orion Nebula. Swirls of green in the Hubble image made from ultraviolet and visible light reveal hydrogen and sulfur gases that have been heated and ionized by intense ultraviolet radiation from young, massive stars. Meanwhile, Spitzer's infrared view, which is rendered as orange and red, exposes carbon-rich molecules called polycyclic aromatic hydrocarbons in the cloud. These representative colors allow us to see this region in a way that vastly expands the limits of our color vision.

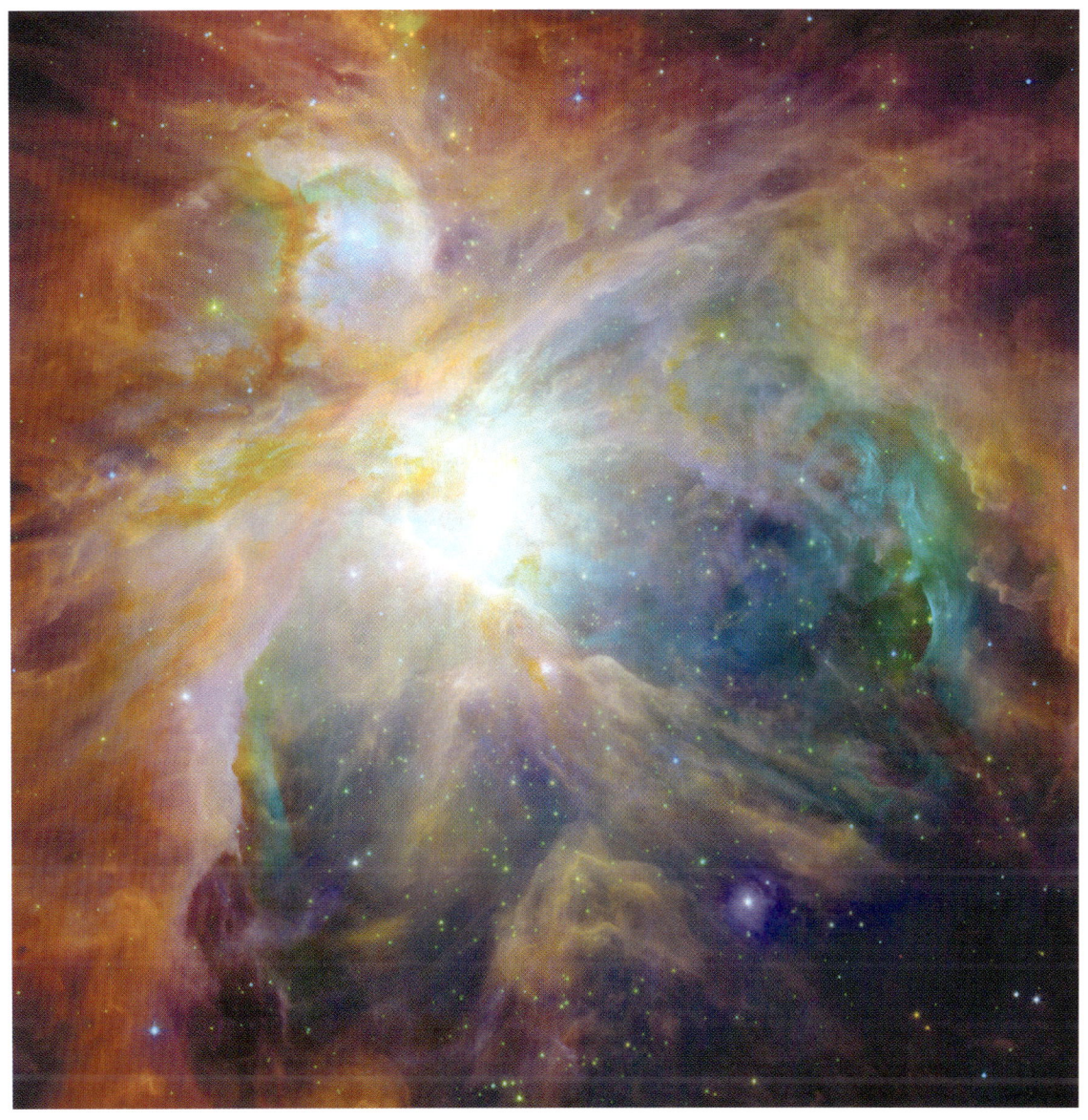

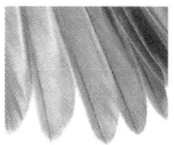

Ted Kinsman

Chickadee in Flight, 2007

Natural science photograph; Canon 20D; high-speed electronic flash

Kinsman Physics Productions, Rochester, New York, United States
and Photo Researchers Inc., New York, New York

This image is the outcome of a series of photographs made of songbirds in flight.
A high-speed capping shutter was used in combination with a high-speed electronic
flash to capture the birds as they approached a bird feeder. An infrared beam was used
to detect the bird and trigger the system. The equipment produced a flash duration of
1/20,000th of a second.

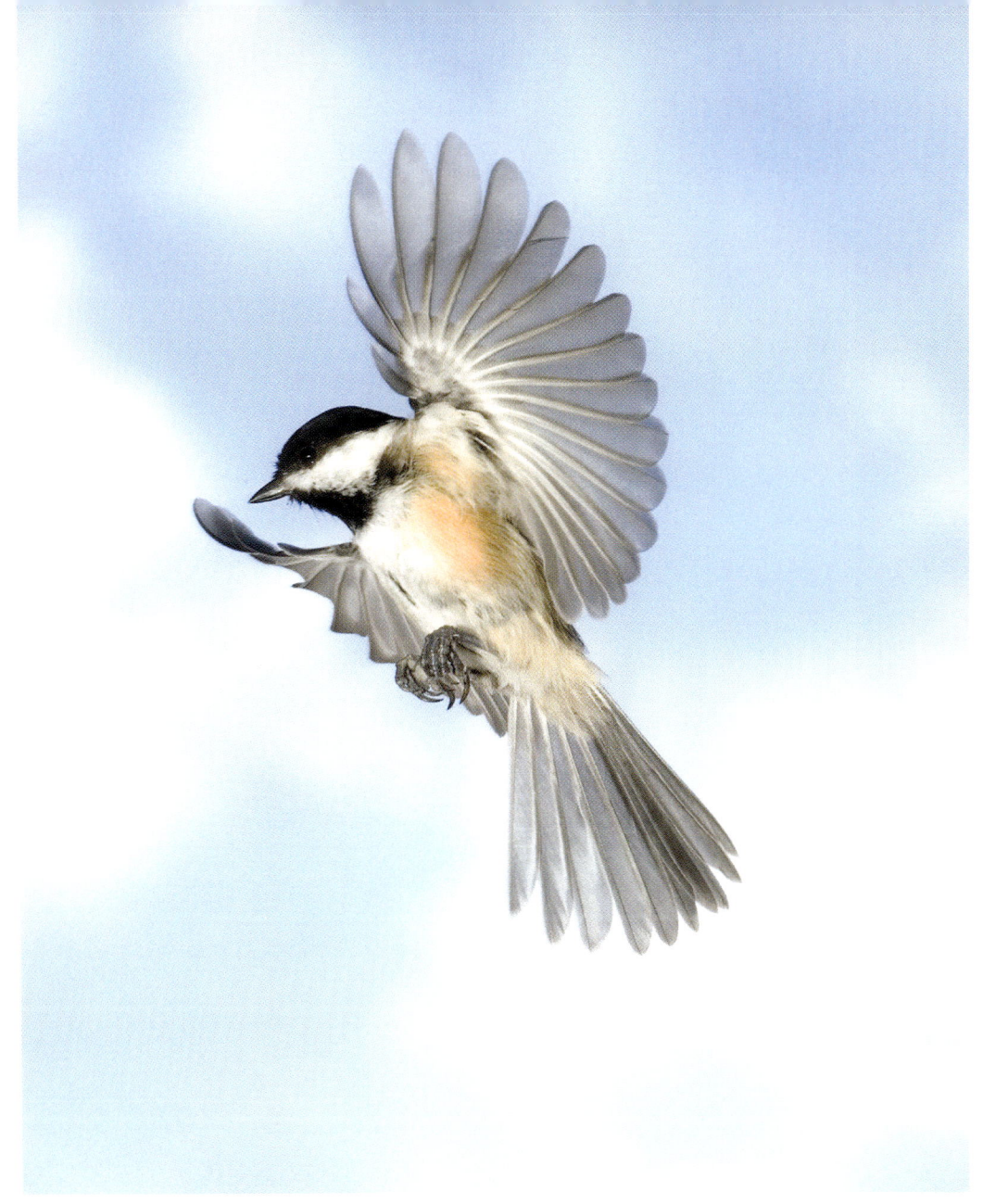

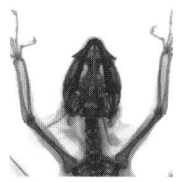

Ted Kinsman

X-Ray of Two Lizards, 2007

Radiograph; initial capture with film; digital scan of a film X-ray image

*Kinsman Physics Productions, Rochester, New York, United States
and Photo Researchers Inc., New York, New York*

This image was made to reveal the boney structure of the reptiles. The reptile located on the left side of the photograph is a flying lizard that uses the bones located in the ribcage as a sail to glide from tree to tree. The reptile on the right is a gecko. The X-ray imaging system that was used would be characterized as a research grade instrument and used low voltage and a 0.5 mm spot size producing a high-resolution image.

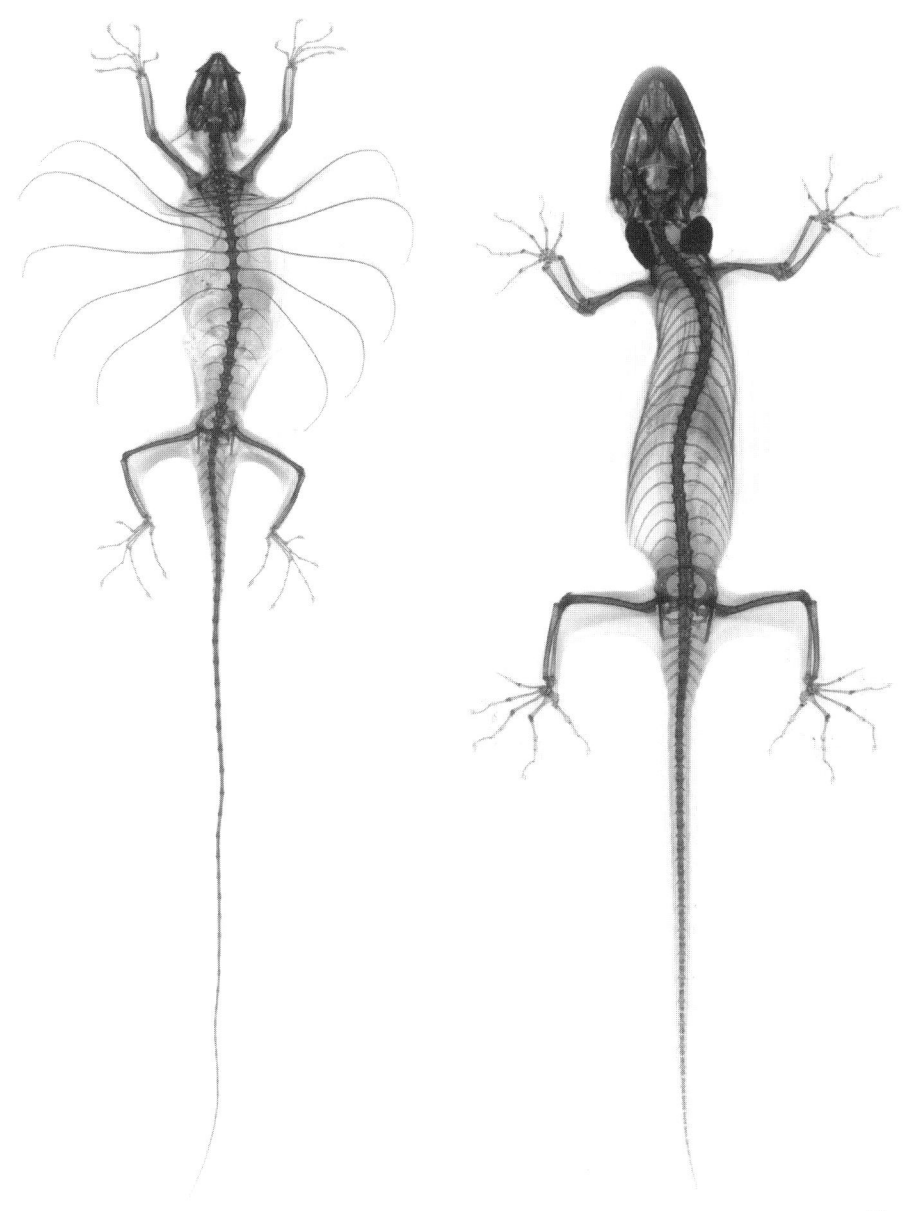

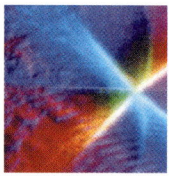

Harald Kleine

Double Blast, 2002

High-speed direction-indicating color schlieren photograph; 35mm color slide film, ISO 400; exposure short duration spark source with open shutter-camera in a darkened room; exposure duration approximately 1 microsecond

School of Aerospace, Civil and Mechanical Engineering, Australian Defense Force Academy, University of New South Wales, Canberra, Australia

Two spherical blast waves, generated by the simultaneous explosion of a pair of identical 10 mg pellets of the high explosive silver azide, interact in mid-air between the two charges. This interaction represents a reflection of the waves from an ideal, non-energy-absorbing surface. At the moment of capture, the reflection pattern became irregular, which is evidenced by the short straight shock segment (the so-called Mach stem) in between the spherical waves. The Mach stem is shown as a ring connecting the two spheres. Simultaneously, the blast front generated by the lower charge reflects from a solid wall, whose surface roughness causes the ripples behind the reflected wave. This reflection should also cause a Mach stem that ideally would be half the size of the one observed in mid-air, but because of energy losses in the reflection process, enhanced by the surface roughness, the formation of this wave was significantly delayed. This image was recorded in the laboratory of Professor K. Takayama, Shock Wave Research Center, Tohoku University, Sendai, Japan.

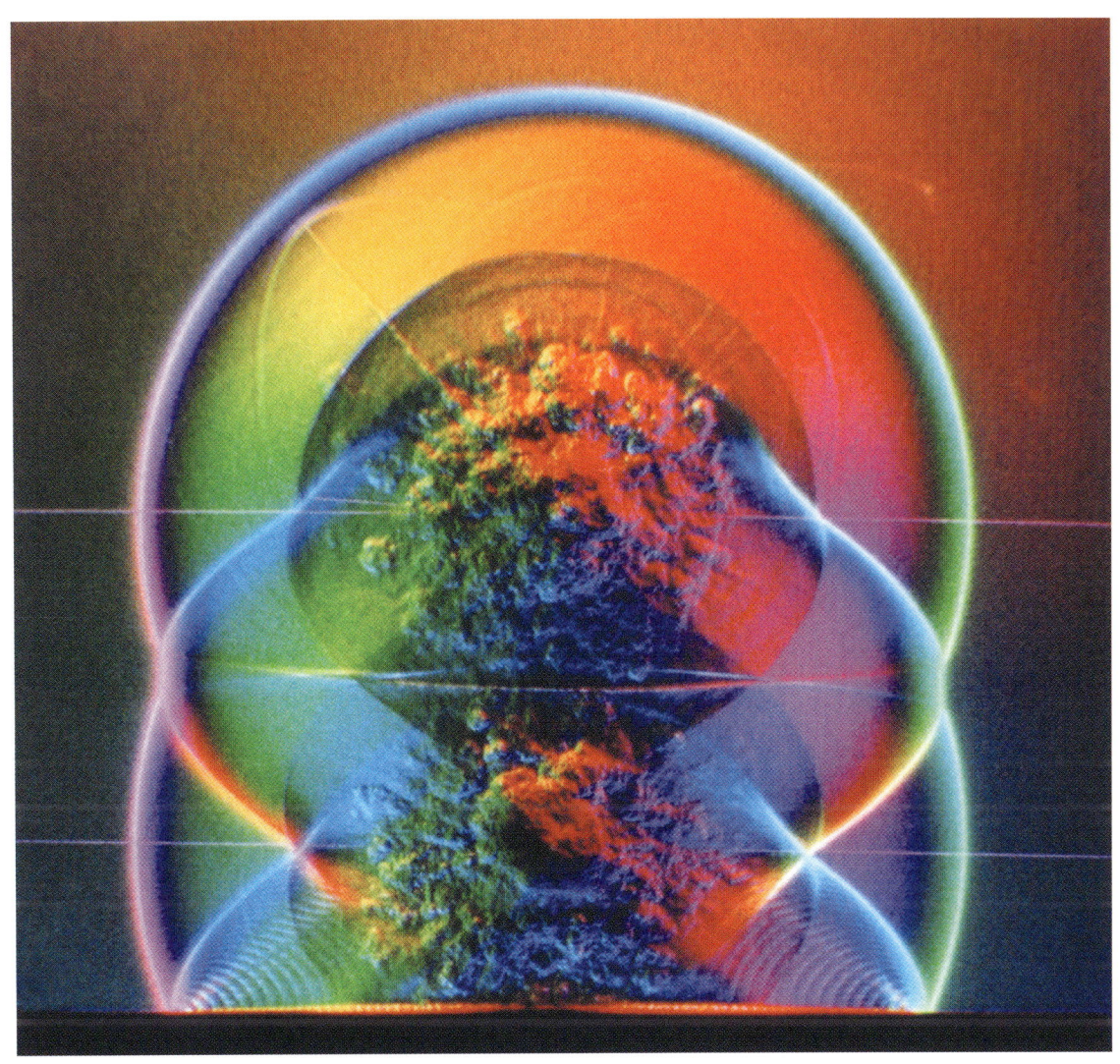

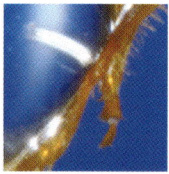

Heidi and Hans-Jürgen Koch

Conditioning Experiment with Honeybee, 2007

Natural science photograph; Nikon D2X, 105 mm Macro lens on a bellows; exposure provided from four synchronized electronic flashes

Animal Affairs Photography, Freiburg, Germany

This honeybee, *Apis mellifera,* is licking a drop of a sugary liquid with its outstretched tongue which was placed at the end of a thin stick. The experiment entailed conditioning the bee to recognize certain scents. In the process, the bee was fixed with tape in a tiny harness and then stimulated with a scent. After the bee had been trained to recognize the odor, it would extend its proboscis—a natural response to locating its normal food, nectar. Scientists in the military have learned that honeybees, which naturally possess an acute sense of smell, can be trained to give the same proboscis reflex action when exposed to vapors commonly used in explosives. This research was carried out at the Julius-Maximilians-Universität in Würzburg, Germany.

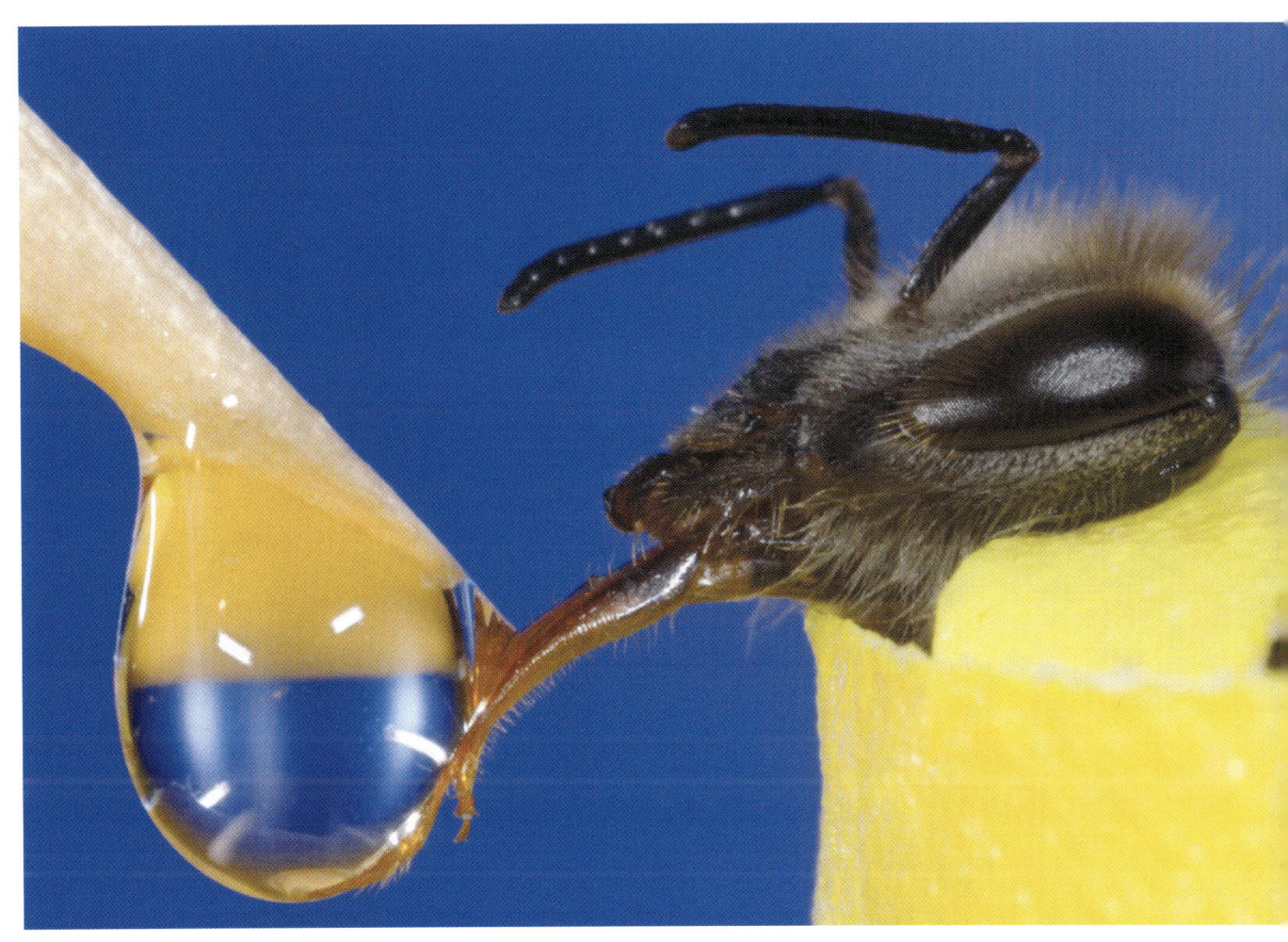

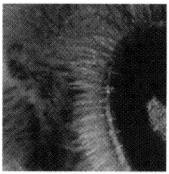

Heidi and Hans-Jürgen Koch

Honeybee with Microchip, 2007

Natural science photograph; Nikon D2X, 105 mm Macro lens on a bellows; exposure provided from two synchronized electronic flashes

Animal Affairs Photography, Freiburg, Germany

This honeybee, feeding on a drop of sugary water had its thorax tagged on with a RFID (radio frequency identification) chip. RFID microchips are often used for monitoring an insect's behavior. The microchip records the individual bee's tag number each time it enters or leaves its hive, thus tracking data about its condition and travel frequency. This research was carried out at the Julius-Maximilians-Universität in Würzburg, Germany.

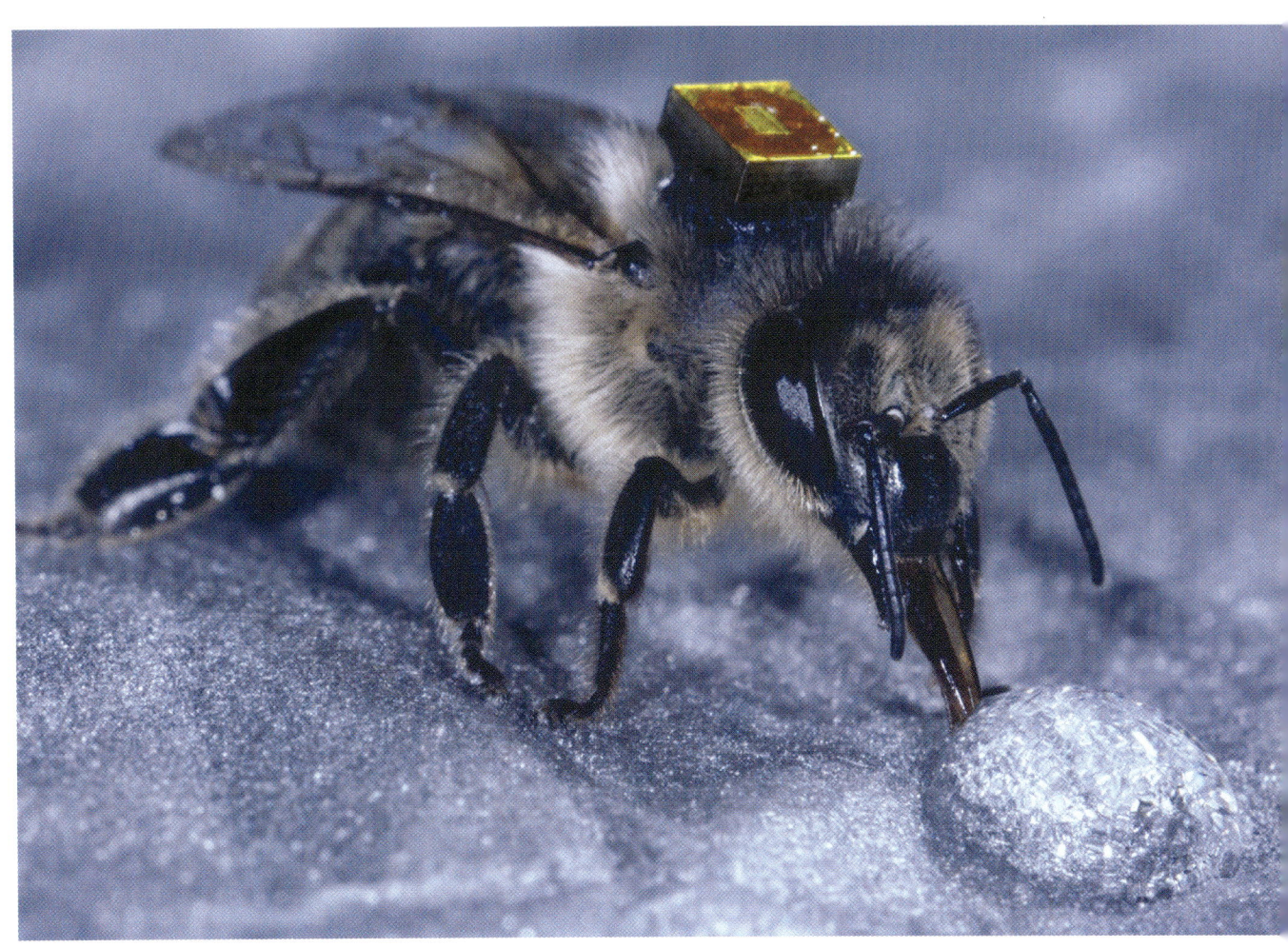

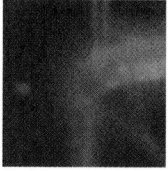

Eugene Kowaluk

Spider Silk Anchoring a Laser Fusion Target, 2006

High-speed photograph; 35mm camera body with a telephoto zoom lens and multiple teleconverters; color negative film

University of Rochester, Laboratory for Laser Energetics, Rochester, New York, United States

An 862 μm-diameter, cryogenic (18.344 K [-426.66°F, -254.81°C]), deuterium-tritium (DT)-fuel spherical capsule was mounted at the center of a 14 mm diameter beryllium "C" mount using four strands of spider silk. The image shows the capsule being irradiated by sixty beams of the OMEGA laser system, raising its temperature to over 100,000,000° C. Individual beam spots, created by each half-trillion-watt beam, can be seen on the target itself. Spider silk was used in mounting the fuel capsule, as it is the stiffest per-unit-mass fiber in existence, minimizing any possible vibration that would affect the laser beam's target accuracy. These experiments in thermonuclear fusion reactions effectively replicate the most basic energy source in the universe—that of stars. A demonstration of ignition in the laboratory is a prerequisite to the commercial production of electricity using thermonuclear fusion.

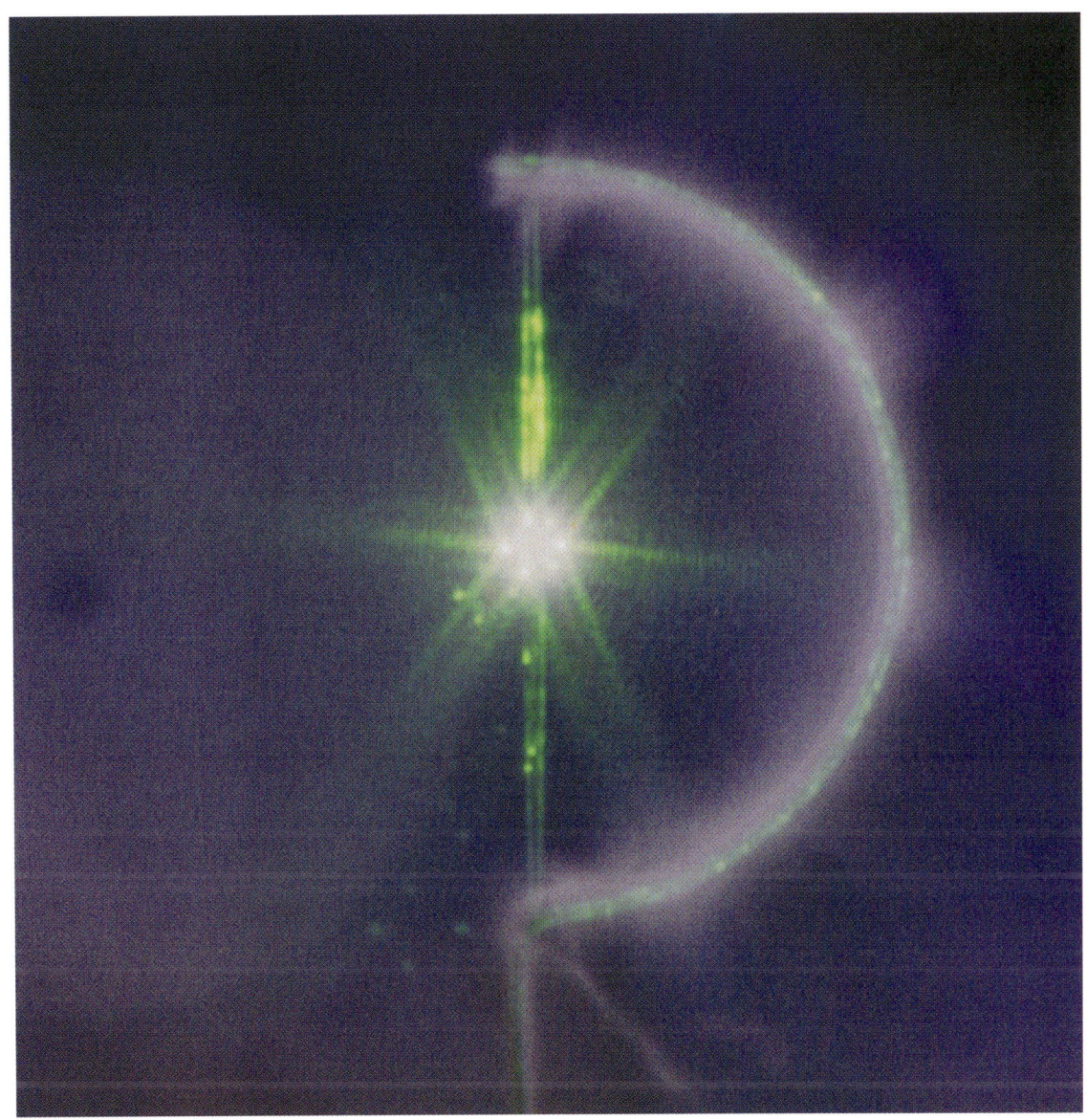

59

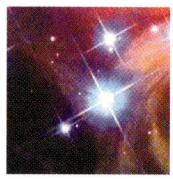

Zoltan Levay

V838 Monocerotis Light Echo, 2004

Astrophotograph; digital exposure using astronomical CCD camera

NASA, European Space Agency (ESA), Association of Universities for Research in Astronomy (AURA), and the Hubble Heritage Team of the Space Telescope Science Institute, Baltimore, Maryland, United States

This image recorded the "light echo" from a sudden brightening of the red supergiant star V838 Monocerotis as it appeared in February 2004. It is one of a series of exposures obtained by the Advanced Camera for Surveys (ACS) aboard NASA's Hubble Space Telescope showing the pulse of light expanding through and illuminating the interstellar medium within a few light-years surrounding the fading star. The color image has been reconstructed from exposures through three broadband filters sampling red/near-infrared, yellow/green, and blue light.

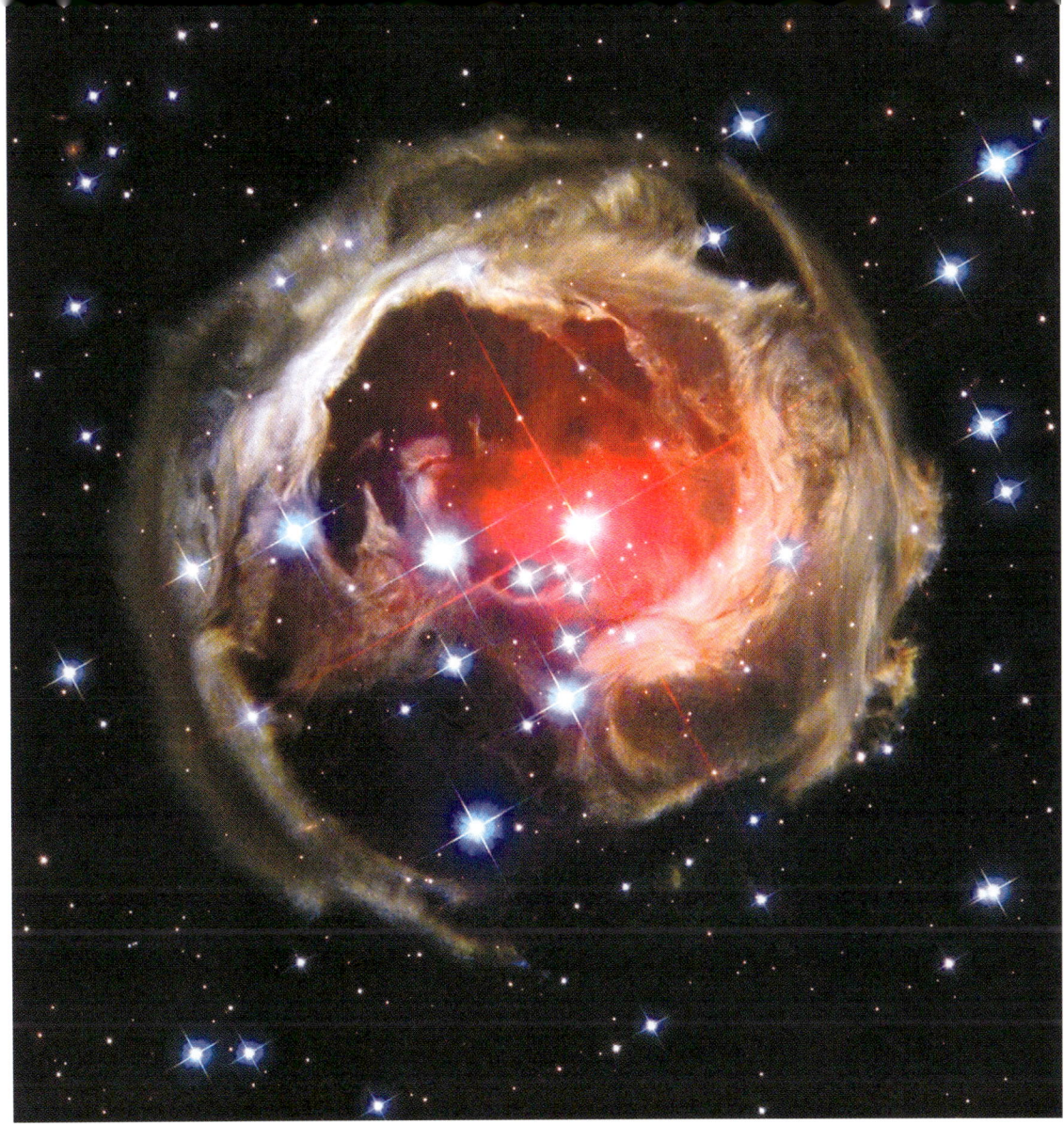

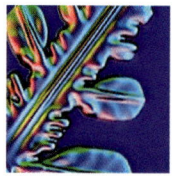

Kenneth Libbrecht

Snow Crystal I, 2006

Photomicrograph; direct digital capture

California Institute of Technology, Physics Department, Pasadena, California, United States

This is a photomicrograph of a natural snow crystal that fell to earth in Cochrane, Ontario. The colors were not digitally created, but were produced by shining colored lights on the crystal from behind. The ice crystal itself acts like a multiple element lens to refract the many different incident colors, producing a rainbow effect. The six-fold symmetry of a snow crystal ultimately derives from the geometry of its constituent water molecules, which hook together to form a hexagonal ice crystal lattice. Small snow crystals first grow into tiny faceted prisms, and often the six corners of a hexagonal plate sprout branches as the crystal grows larger. Because the six branches all experience the same temperature and humidity as the crystal tumbles through the clouds, they all grow in synchrony, producing the snowflake's distinctive, symmetrical appearance.

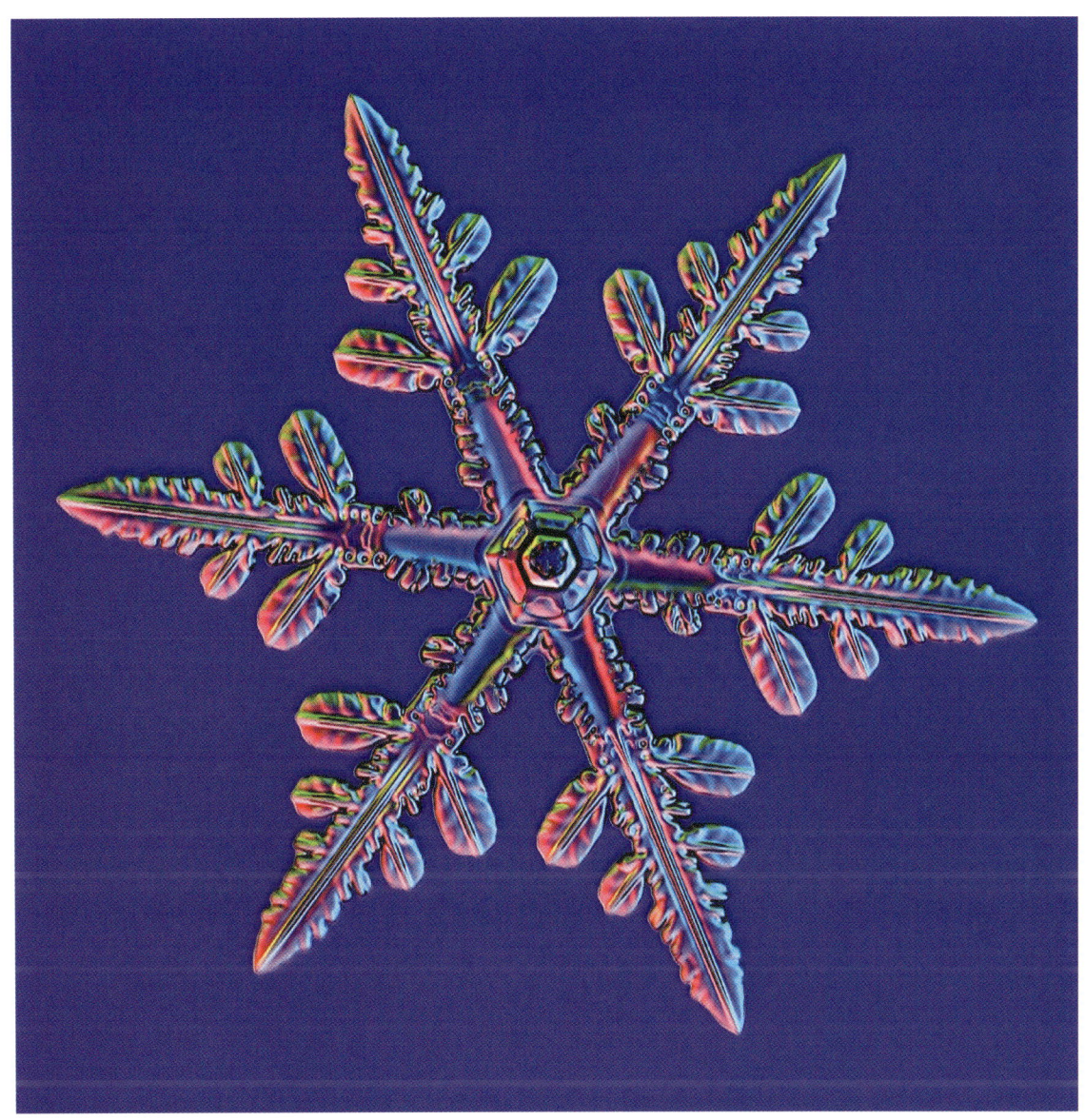

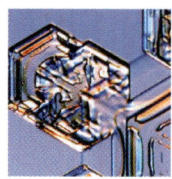

Kenneth Libbrecht

Snow Crystal II, 2004

Photomicrograph; direct digital capture

California Institute of Technology, Physics Department, Pasadena, California, United States

This photomicrograph reveals a natural snow crystal that fell to earth in Burlington, Vermont, measuring just over 3 mm (0.12 inches) from tip-to-tip. Snow crystals grow into a wide variety of shapes, ranging from thin, plate-like crystals to slender hexagonal columns (the same basic shape as wooden pencils), depending mainly on the temperature in which they grow. If a crystal experiences a range of temperatures as it falls, it may grow into a column capped with two plates, or into a thick plate made of several ice layers. If you look carefully, you can see four distinct layers in this snow crystal.

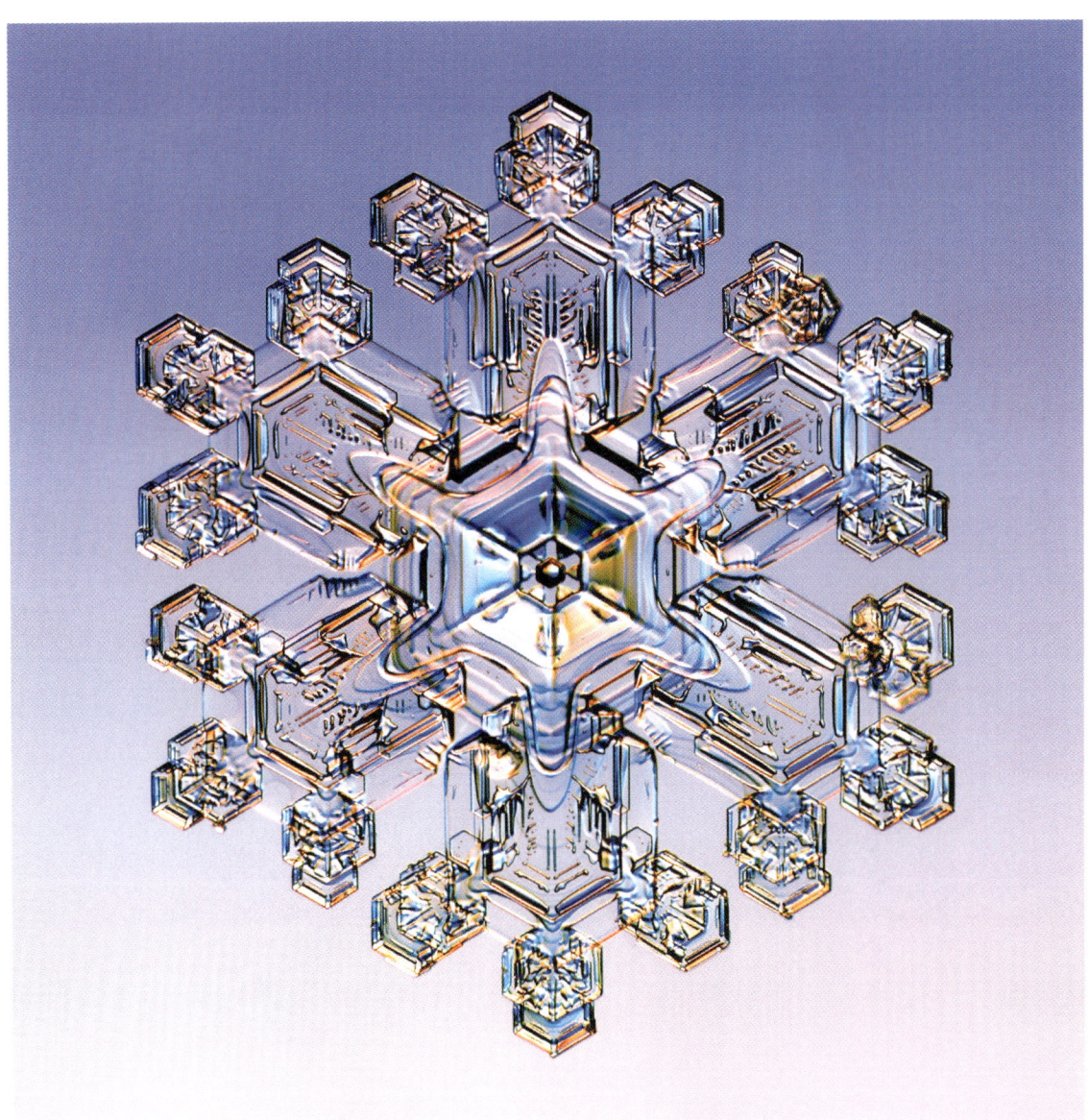

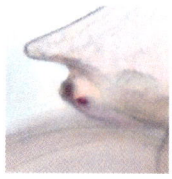

Kevin Mackenzie

Lips, 2006

Photomicrograph; Zeiss Axioskop; 40 + Progress C14 digital camera

University of Aberdeen, Microscopy and Cellular Imaging Facility,
Institute of Medical Sciences, Aberdeen, Scotland

The common water flea, of the family *Daphniidae*, is found in most bodies of fresh water. It is a valuable food source for animals such as fish and newts. The water flea's transparent body offers a clear view of all their body systems, which makes them an ideal subject for microscopical examination using brightfield illumination. The water flea depicted here has just eaten a meal of green algae that appears as a green line throughout the animal's digestive tract. This close up of the head also reveals the flea's wispy antennae at top, a large compound eye (appears as a dark spot), and a beak-like mouth observed at the left.

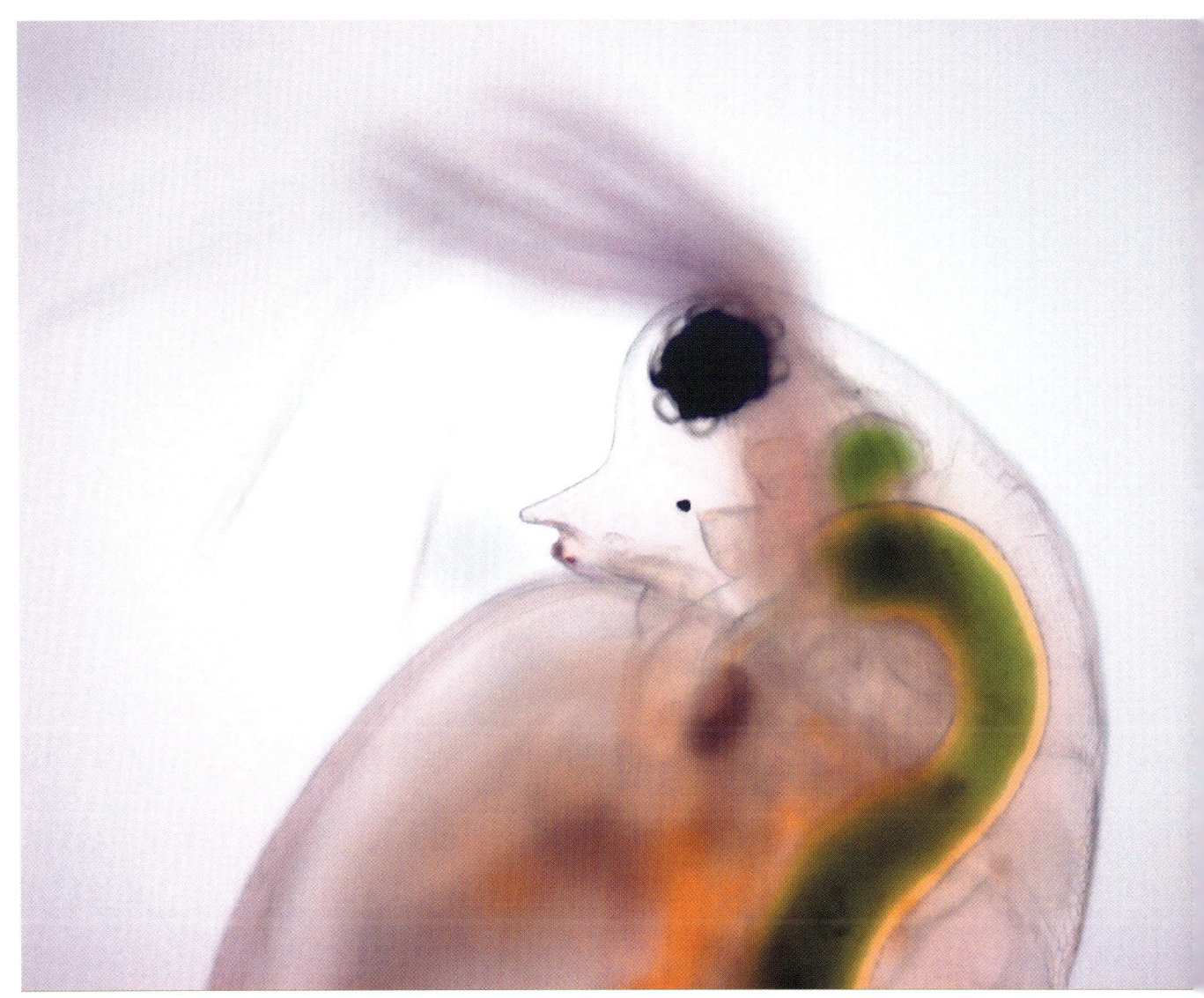

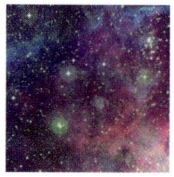

David Malin

The Carina Nebula, False Color, Narrow Band Image

Original plates exposed in 1979–1980; image produced in 2008
Astrophotograph; UK Schmidt Telescope of the Anglo-Australian Observatory

Anglo-Australian Observatory, Eastwood, Australia

The Great Nebula in Carina is 7,000 light-years away but is easily visible to the unaided eye. It contains vast amounts of gas and dust and many very hot stars. Their ultraviolet radiation ionizes the gas, which emits narrow, monochromatic emission lines characteristic of the constituent elements. This image combines the light of two separate emission lines of oxygen in the UV and green parts of the spectrum with a strong red line from sulfur, using arbitrary colors to aid interpretation.

This image was made by exposing three individual glass plate negatives using narrow band filters to isolate [OII, 373nm], [OIII, 501nm] and [SII, 672nm] emission lines (singly and doubly ionized oxygen and singly ionized sulphur). The plates were contact printed onto film using unsharp masks to control contrast. The positives were scanned and registered to create RGB channels in Photoshop CS3, where R = [OIII], G = [SII] and B = [OII].

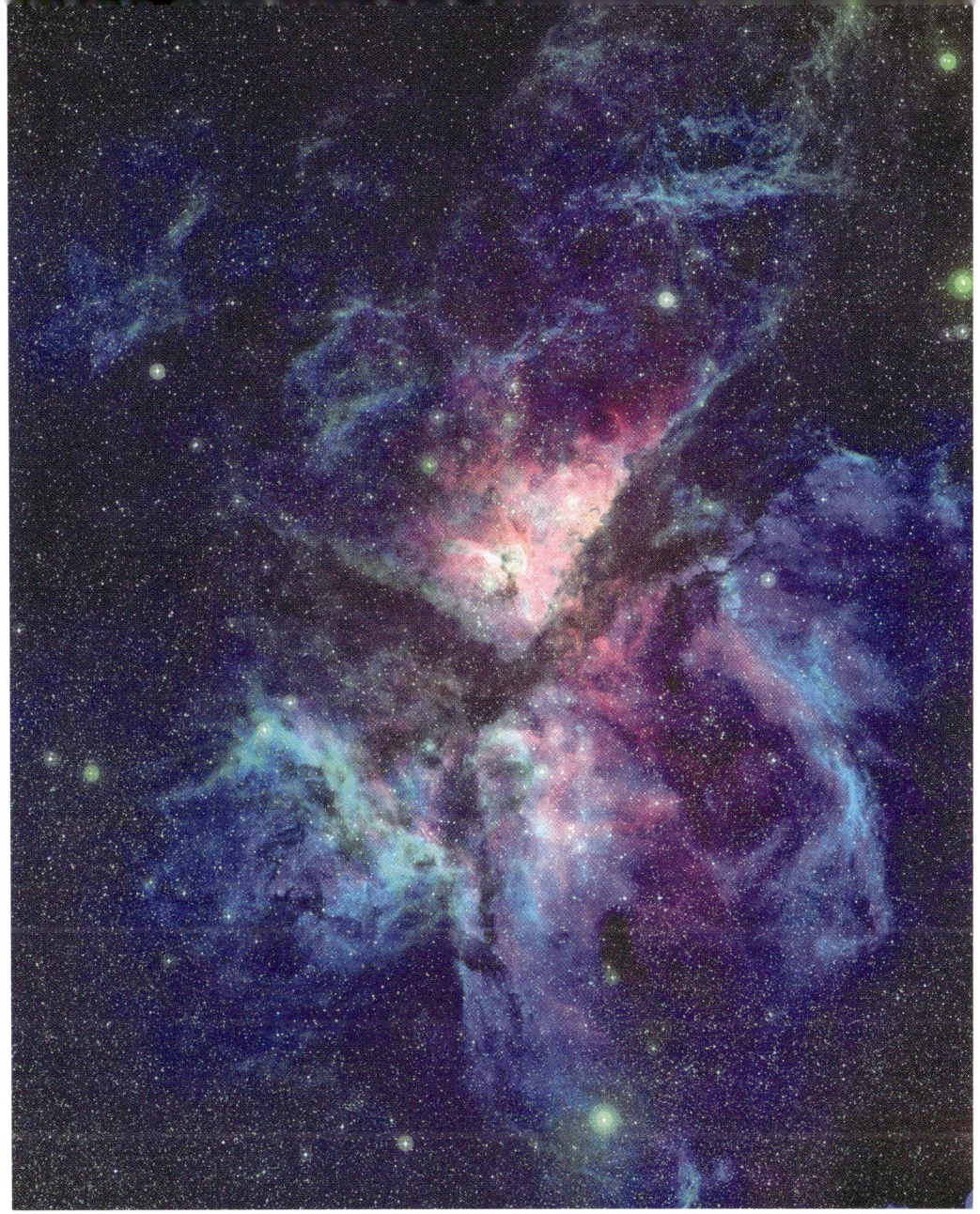

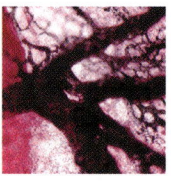

Shannon McCook

48-Hour Chick Embryo: Brightfield, 2006

Photomicrograph; magnification approximately ×12 at capture;
direct digital capture using a SPOT II camera

*Biomedical Photographic Communications, Rochester Institute of Technology,
Rochester, New York, United States*

This photograph is a chicken embryo injected with India ink at the 48th hour of
development. The whole organism was mounted on a slide for examination, which
would be described as a whole mount. This photograph is comprised of over 250
individual images used to create a map of the specimen. Because of thickness and
the requirement for image depth of field, approximately 2–3 images were exposed at
varying image depths across each 1-micrometer distance of the embryo to provide for
maximum depth of field and resolution in the final photograph. These images were
then digitally merged using Adobe PhotoShop® to create the final composite picture.

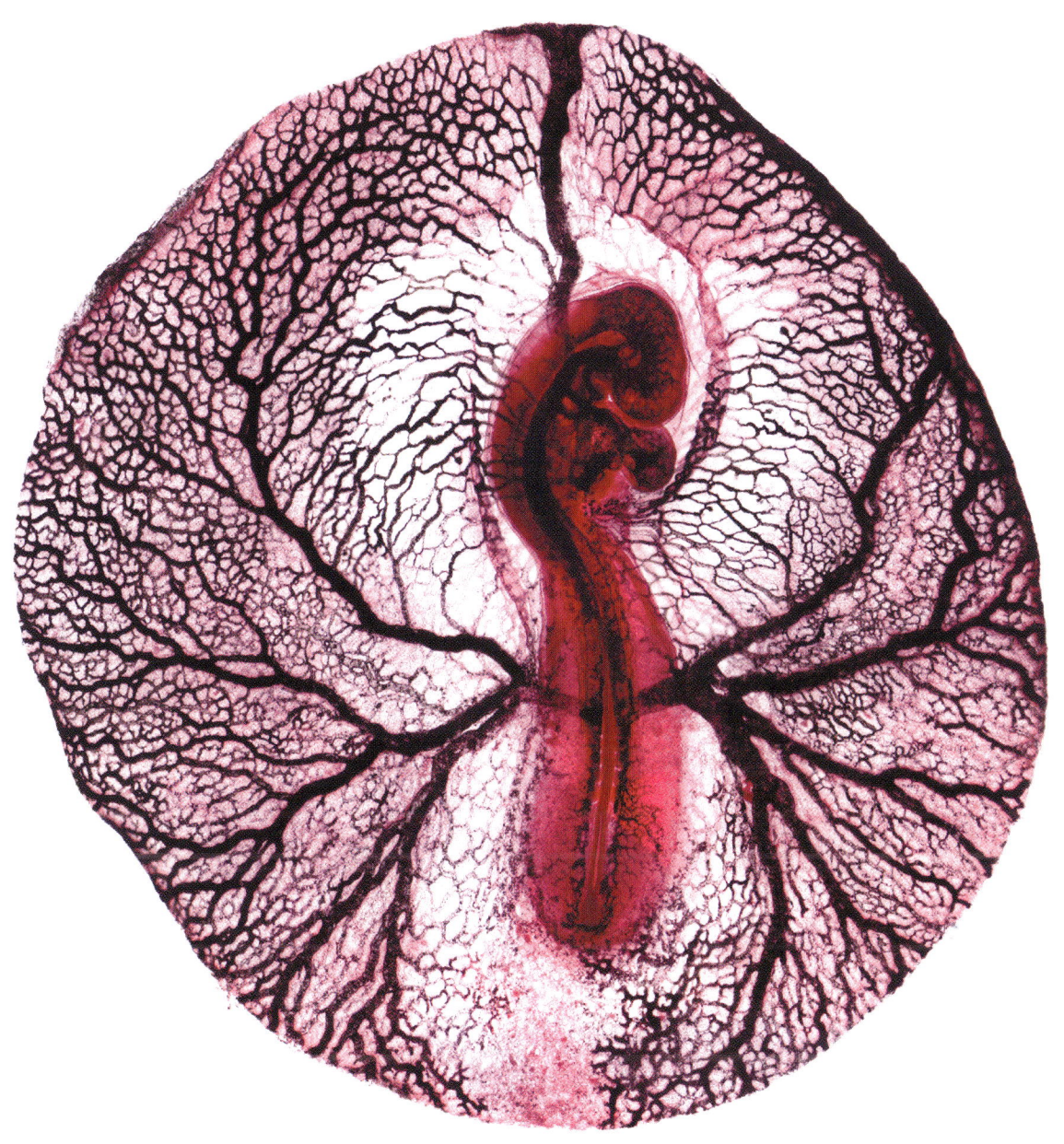

71

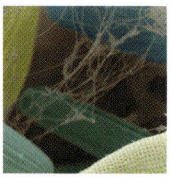

Oliver Meckes and Nicole Ottawa

Stromatolite, 2007

Scanning electron photomicrograph; magnification approximately ×600 at capture; post-capture digital colorization

Eye of Science, Reutlingen, Germany

Stromatolites are mineralized microbial communities, formed from cyanobacteria, (formerly known as blue-green algae). Their formation takes thousands of years as the cyanobacteria trap detritus and sediment, forming large living rafts known as microbial mats. The cyanobacteria also secrete calcium carbonate, which causes the mats to mineralize, forming layered rock-like structures. This sample was taken from Lake Thetis, a saline lake in Western Australia.

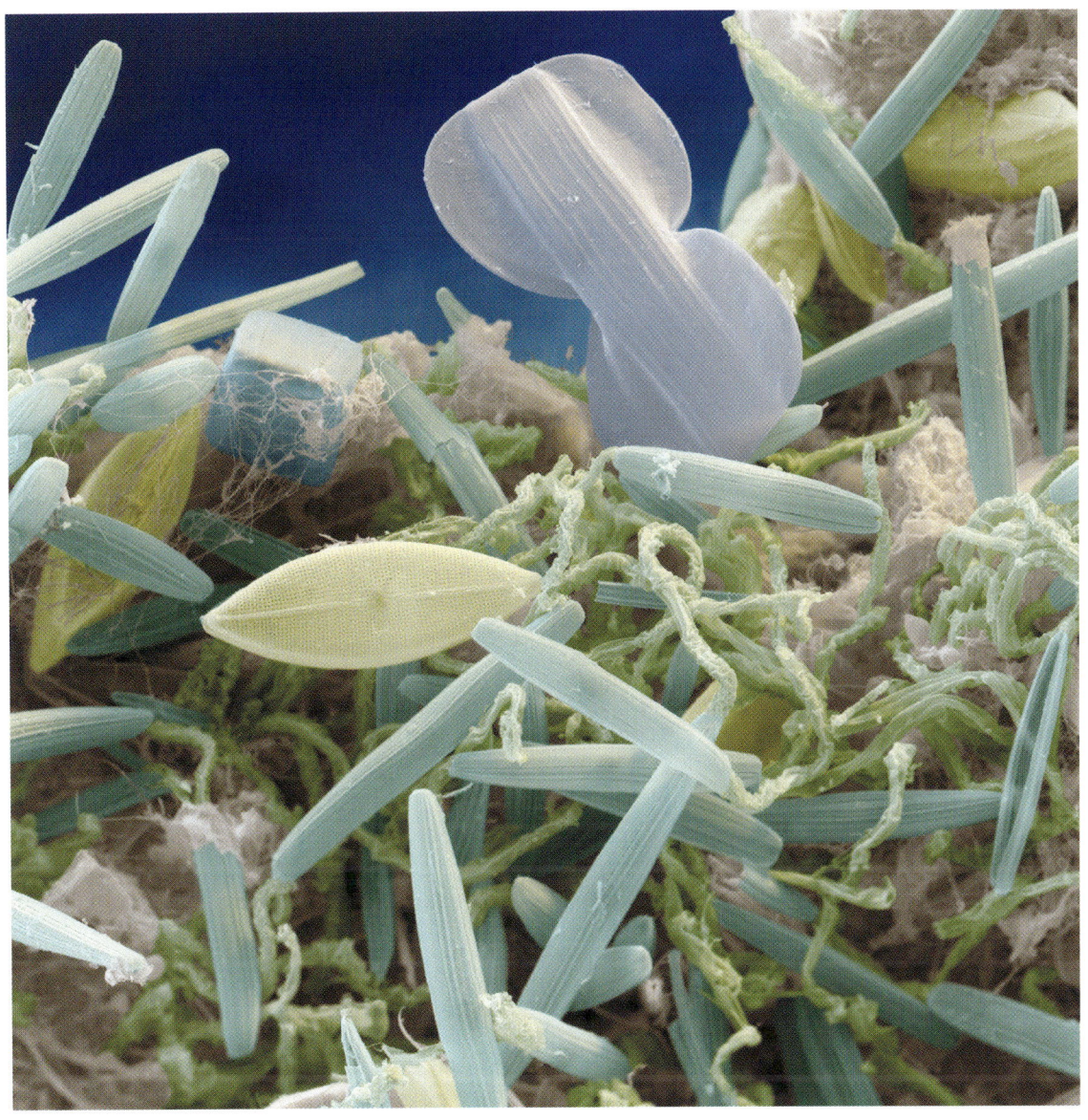

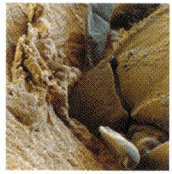

Oliver Meckes and Nicole Ottawa

Zecke in Haut, 2007

Scanning electron photomicrograph; magnification approximately ×50 at capture; post-capture digital colorization

Eye of Science, Reutlingen, Germany

This colored scanning electron micrograph (SEM) of a tick, *Ixodes sp.*, shows its mouthparts buried in the skin of a human host while feeding on blood. The legs are protruding from the body on either side of the insect where the tick is embedded in the skin. A shield-like plate on the back of the body, (colored brown on the left), characterizes this genus of hard-bodied ticks. Ticks are vectors for a number of diseases caused by bacteria or viruses, including Lyme disease, tick-borne encephalitis (TBE), tick typhus, and Colorado tick fever.

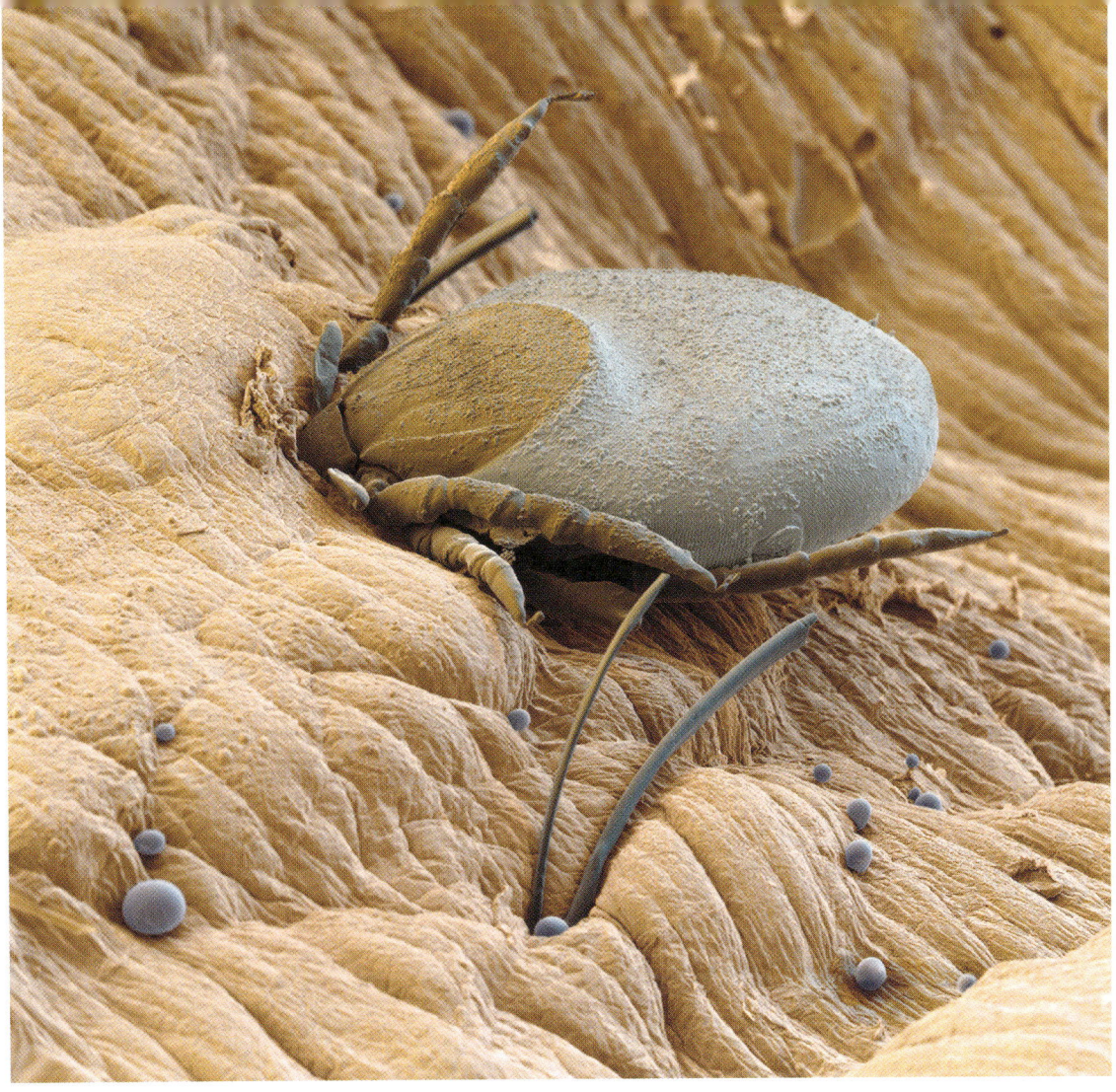

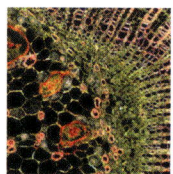

Torey Miller

Tilia (Linden), Darkfield, 2008

Photomicrograph; Olympus compound darkfield photomicroscope; magnification approximately ×10 at capture; direct digital capture using a SPOT II camera

Biomedical Photographic Communications, Rochester Institute of Technology, Rochester, New York, United States

This photomicrograph shows a sample of *Tilia sp.* (Linden), a botanical specimen with unique, circular structures. The microscope used to make the image was outfitted with darkfield condenser because it best delineated the internal structures that would otherwise be transparent in traditional brightfield illumination microscopy. Many individual images were captured and have been stitched together to make up this composite photograph, which exhibits high structural detail and resolution.

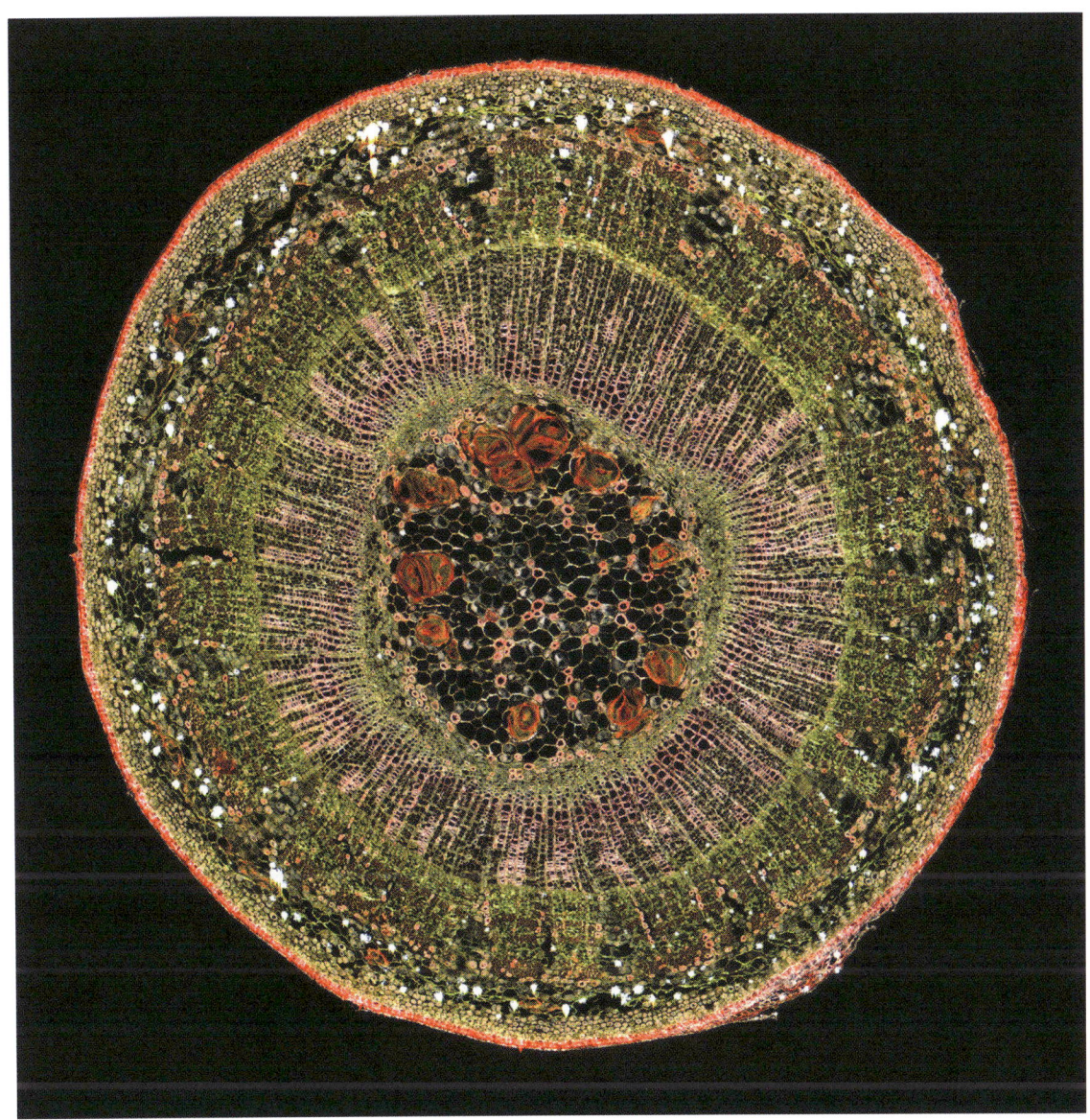

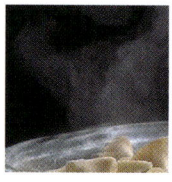

Joe Ogrodnick

Sclerotinia sclerotiorum: Ejection of Ascospores, 2006

Natural Science Photograph; digital SLR capture; modified darkfield illumination using electronic flash

New York State Agricultural Experiment Station, Cornell University, Geneva, New York, United States

This photograph reveals the ejection of mature ascospores by the apothecia (mushrooms) of the fungus *Sclerotinia sclerotiorum* in response to reduction of the relative humidity and changes in air pressure (osmotic pressure or potential) achieved by removing the petri dish cover. The ascospores are so small and numerous, they appear as smoke in this photograph.

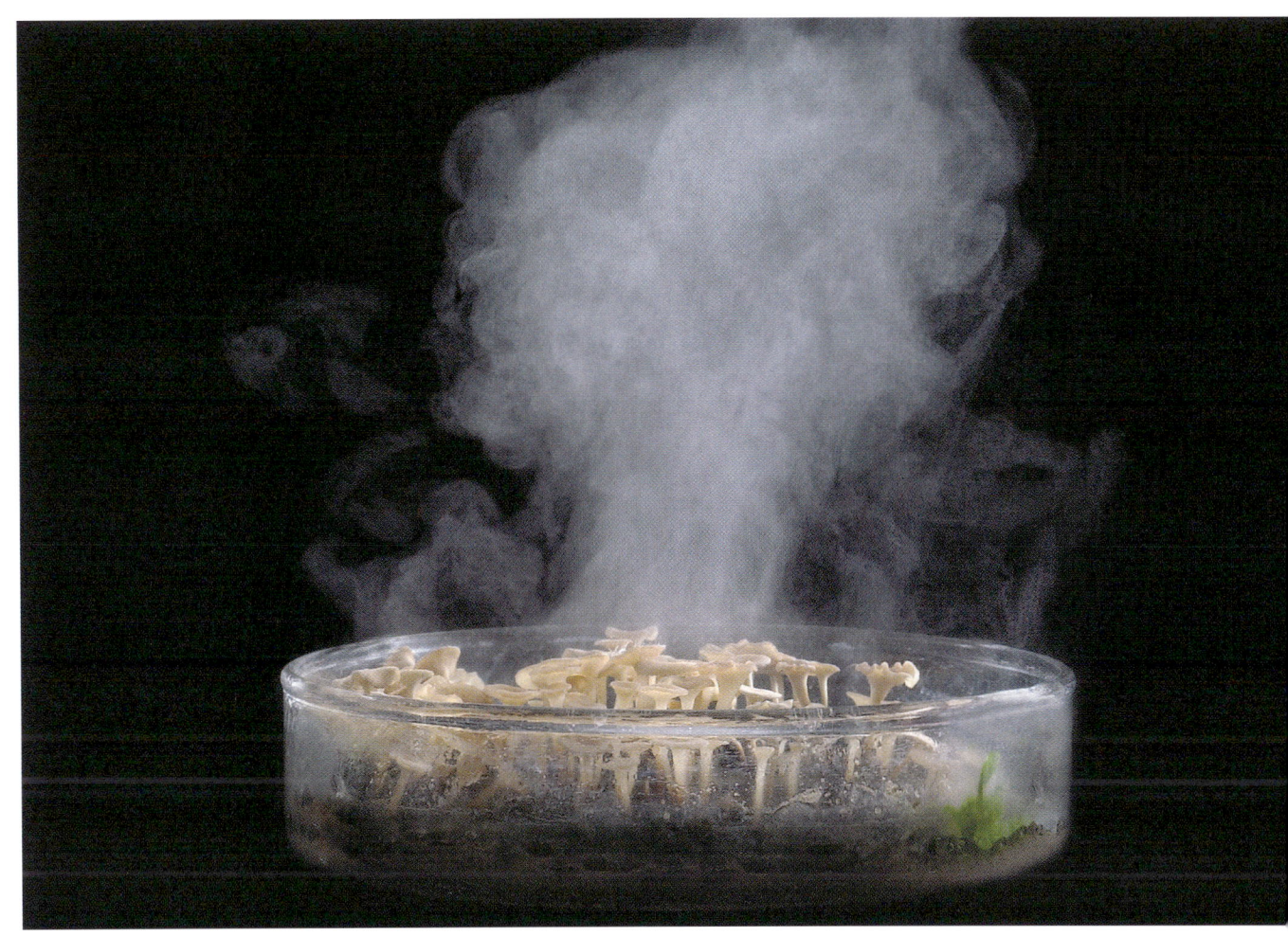

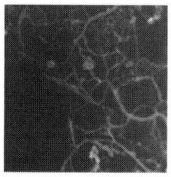

Jim R. Oramas

Retinal Blood Vessels Gone Wild, 2006

Fundus photograph; Topcon TRC 50EX retinal camera with OIS digital capture

Bascom Palmer Eye Institute, Miami, Florida, United States

This frame of a fluorescein angiogram shows an advanced case of diabetic retinopathy, with extensive neo-vascularization, areas of non-perfusion and a fibrous vascular tissue that extends along the superior arcade into the vitreous. Diabetic retinopathy is a pathologic condition, characterized by a series of progressive retinal changes caused by long standing diabetes. The disease is composed of two stages known as early (non-proliferative) or advanced (proliferative) retinopathy. In the early stages of retinopathy, common findings include micro-aneurysms, hemorrhages, exudates, and dilation of retinal veins. In the advanced stages of proliferative retinopathy as seen on this photo, the disease moves into a more aggressive state, adding the growth of new blood vessels due to lack of oxygen to the eye. This process is known as neo-vascularization. Also seen in advanced stages of proliferative retinopathy is the formation of connecting scar tissue, which is referred to as fibrous vascular tissue. Along with the above-mentioned conditions, all of these states can cause extremely poor vision.

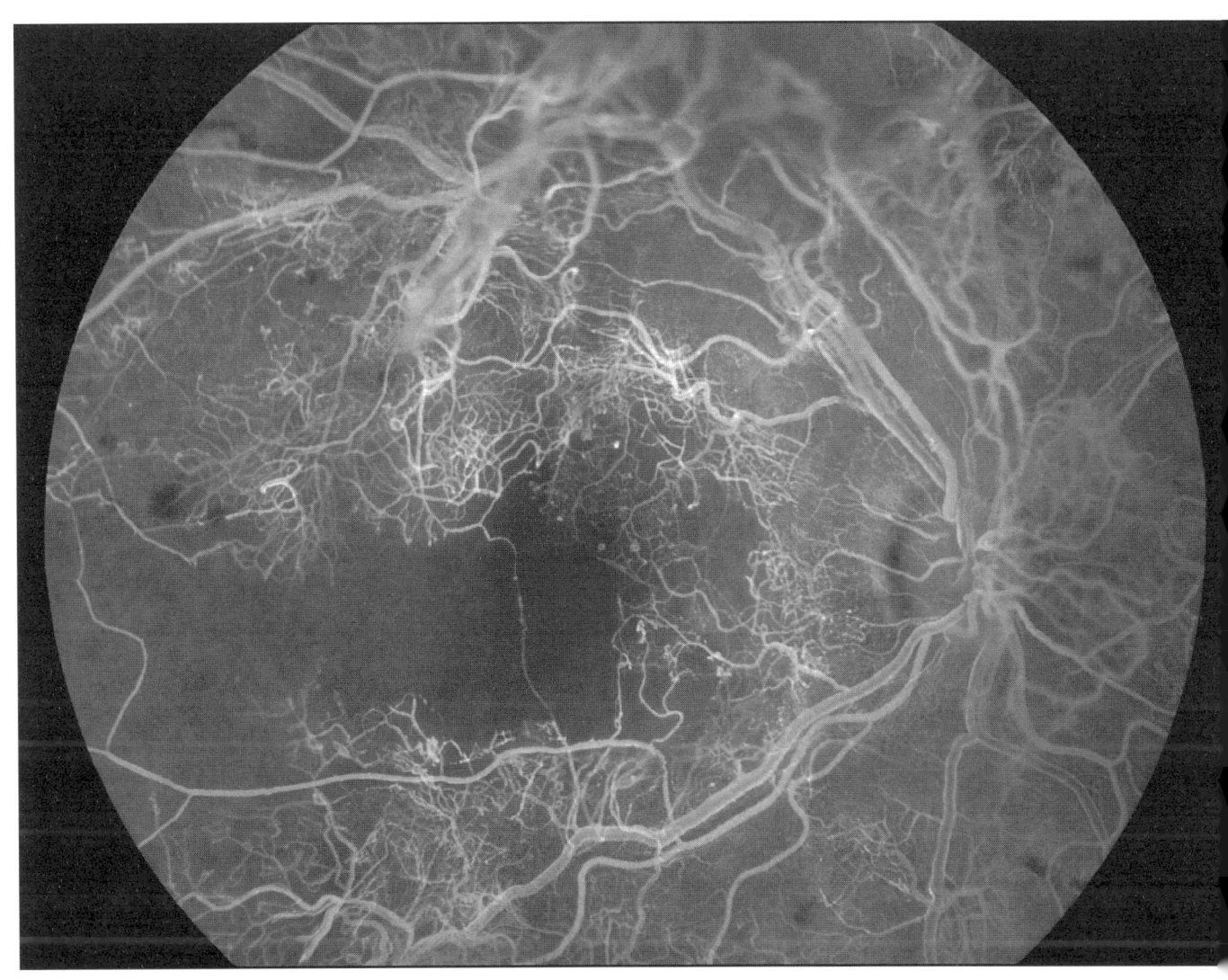

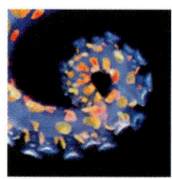

David Paul

Octopus Paralarvae, 2000

Natural science photograph; 35mm camera; Fuji Velvia film

dpimages, Victoria, Australia

Photographed in the Coral Sea, Far North Queensland, this octopus paralarvae is a pelagic juvenile of an unknown species collected at night over deep water. On moonless nights, small planktonic marine life migrate to the surface to feed. They can be found by doing a "black water hang," diving behind the boat on a rope and viewing at close proximity with peripheral flashlight for illumination. The creature's actual size is about 15 mm from the top to bottom— or the length of its mantle, or body.

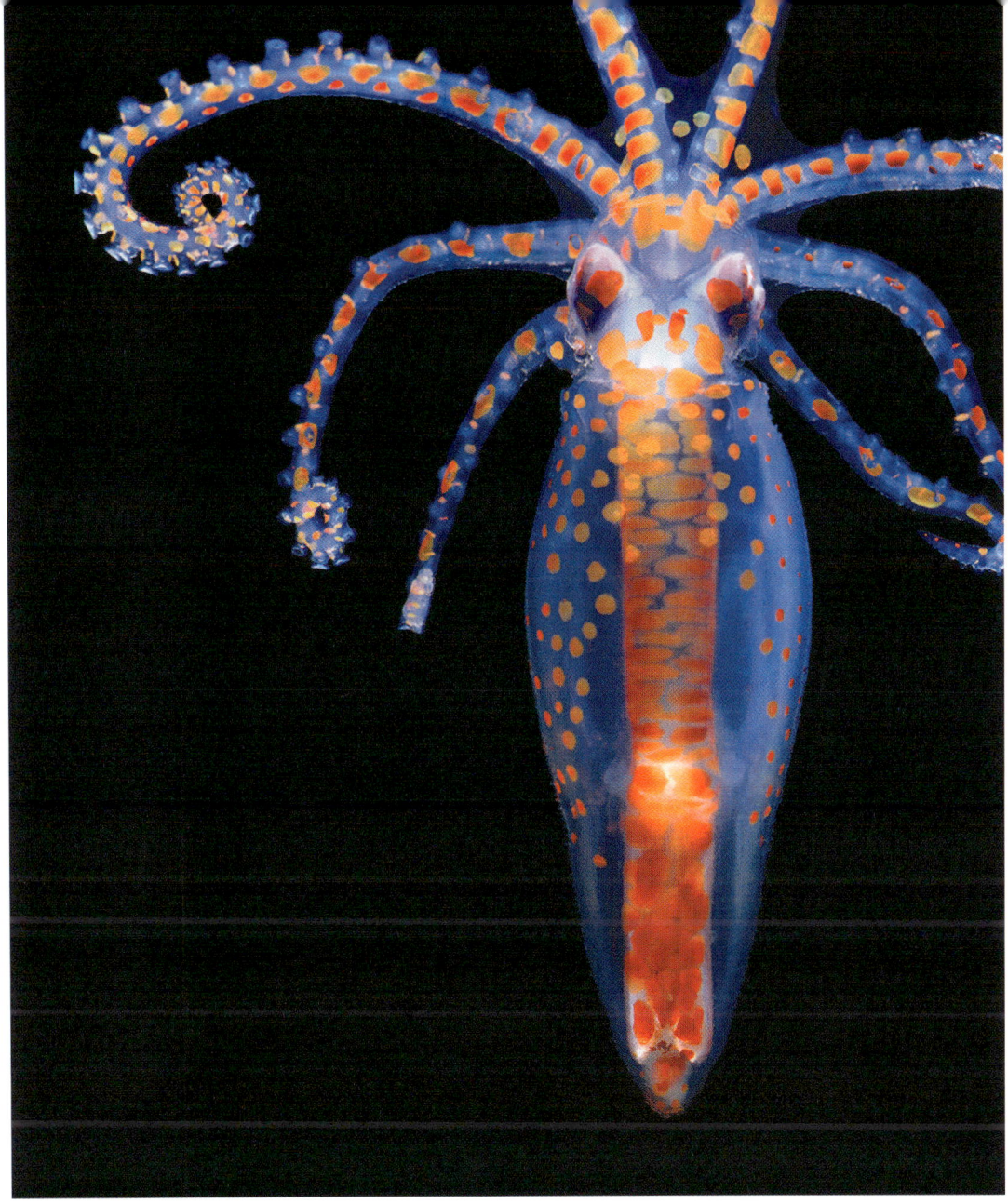

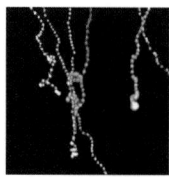

David Paul

Gabo Jelly, 2003

Natural science photograph; 35mm camera; Fuji Velvia film

dpimages, Victoria, Australia

This photograph was made on the remote Gabo Island off the coast of Southern Australia on the border of Victoria and New South Wales. Gabo Island has a pristine marine environment. It is occupied only by its lighthouse, which is used to monitor weather patterns. The Gabo jelly is a bell type of unknown species. It was quite small and delicate, (about 10 mm across the bell), and illuminated by flashlight to enable focusing. A tethered strobe from the same direction as the flashlight was used to create an inner glow from the jelly substance. Capturing the delicate form of the tentacles was a matter of patience and luck.

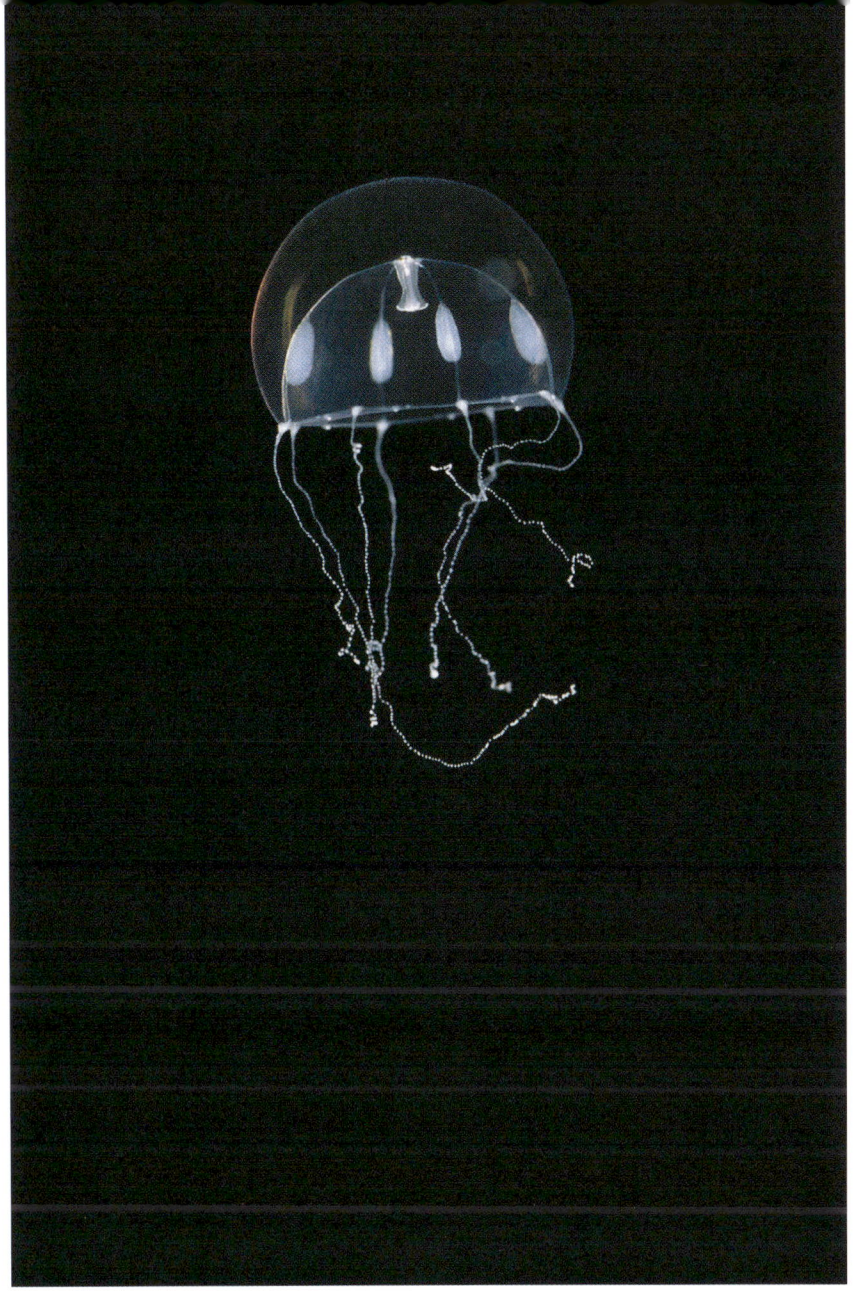

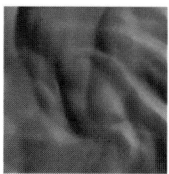

Phred Petersen

Camp stove, 2008

High-speed schlieren photograph; direct capture onto 8 × 10 Ilford HP 5 film using Broncolor Grafit 2 flash equipment; flash duration of approximately 250 microseconds (1/4000 sec.)

RMIT University, Melbourne, Australia

Using a schlieren imaging system, the heat produced from a gas-fueled backpacking stove rises around a small cooking pan becomes visible. In this photograph, a slit light source was used in a Z-type schlieren arrangement which incorporated two 300mm f/10 mirrors. Schlieren are inhomogeneities in transparent material and are not visible to the human eye. They may be characterized as differences in optical path lengths that cause energy travel to be deviated. This deviation is observed as shadows in a schlieren system. A stop was used to the control sensitivity of the system.

The image was recorded at a life size because the system had no lens and both the subject and the film plane were located six meters from the second schlieren mirror. An electronic flash with a flash duration of approximately 250 microseconds was used to freeze the high-speed event.

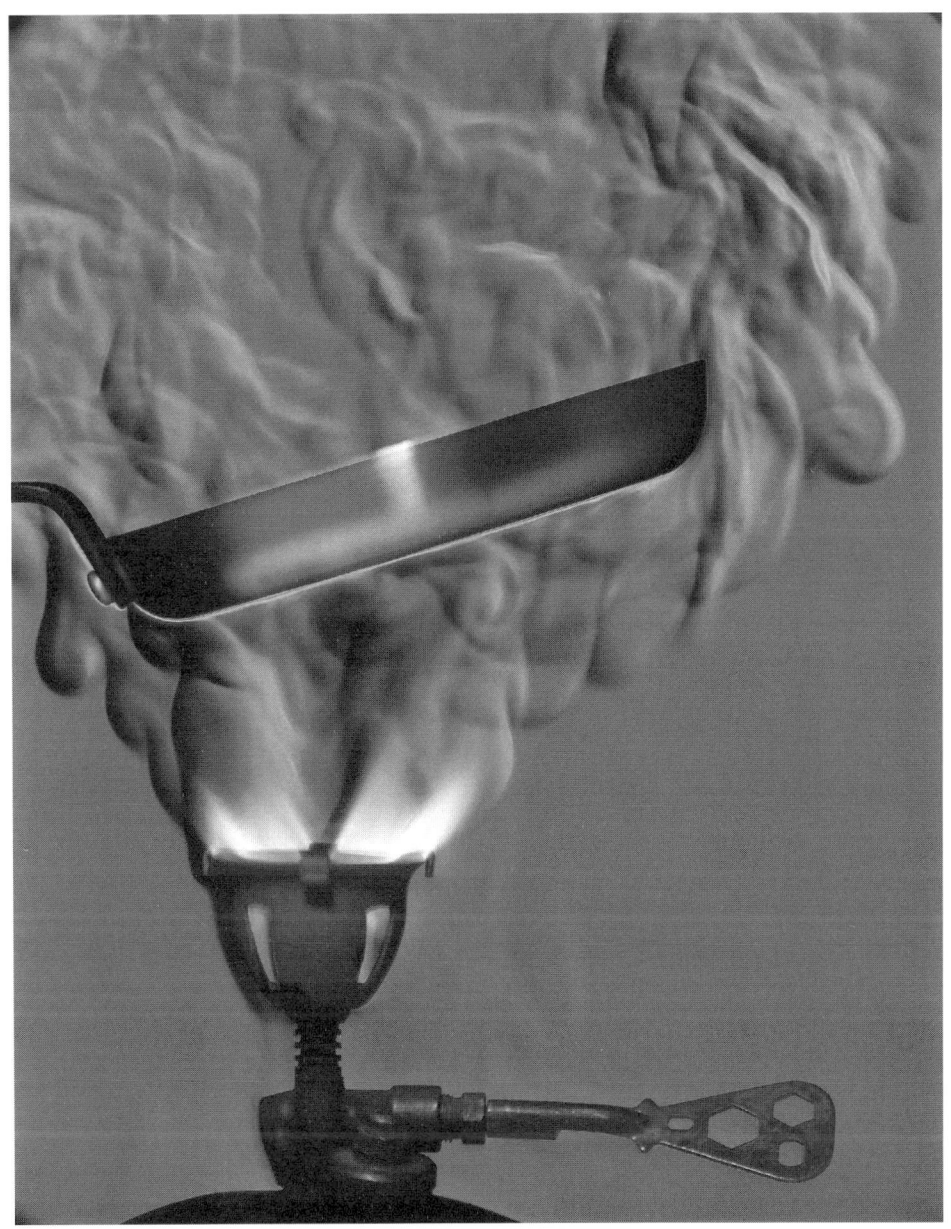

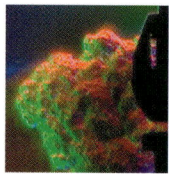

Phred Petersen

Pop rocket, 2007

High-speed schlieren photograph; Canon 350D camera with a 210 mm lens and Hadland Microflash unit; flash duration approximately 5 microseconds (1/200,000 sec.)

RMIT University, Melbourne, Australia

This photograph recorded the blast wave produced from a toy rocket that was tipped with a cap gun charge. The visibility of an event that would normally be invisible to eye is the result of contrast from the schlieren imaging system and high-speed flash. A perforated metal plate below the impact point partially reflects the wave, which allows multiple wave fronts to pass through the perforations and recombine below. The combustion gases of the small explosion are shown to move at a much lower velocity than the blast wave itself.

A three-color circular light source was used in a Z-type schlieren arrangement with two 300mm f/10 mirrors. An adjustable iris was used in the cutoff plane to control sensitivity of the system.

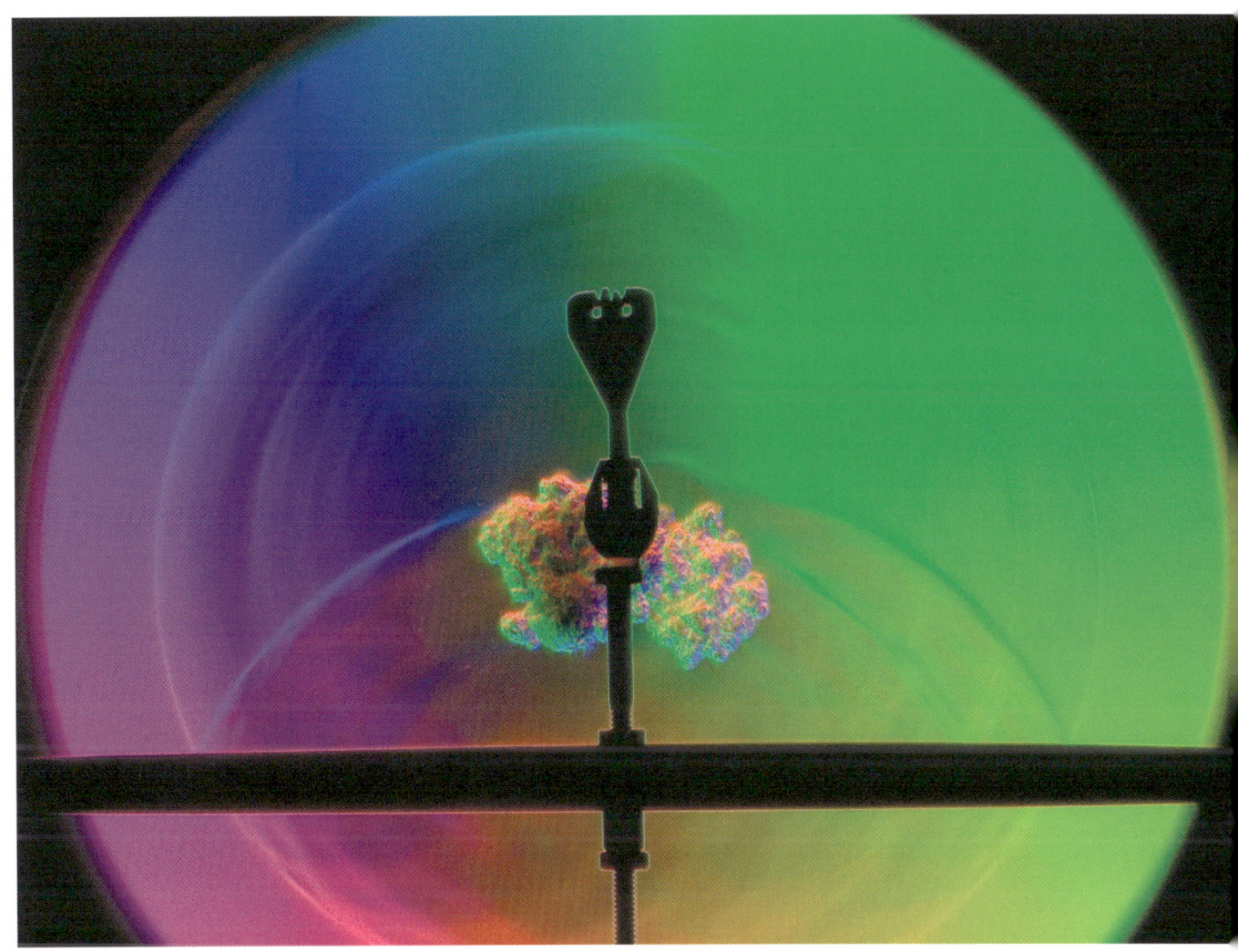

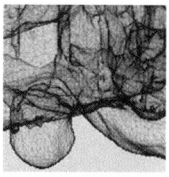

Seth Ruffins

Brain Mesh, 2006

Digital Scientific Image; digital rendering derived from
magnetic resonance imaging (MRI) system images

California Institute of Technology, Pasadena, California, United States

These two views of a wireframe surface model are derived from an MRI atlas of an adult mouse brain. The surface models show the boundaries of approximately 30 identified anatomical structures comprising the brain including the eyes and optic nerves, cerebral cortex, cerebellum, hippocampus, anterior commissure, trigeminal ganglia and nerve roots, and the brain stem. Brain anatomy was manually delineated from Diffusion Weighted Image MRI (not shown) collected by J. Michael Tyszka with a 11.7 Tesla Bruker MRI scanner at the Beckman Institute Biological Imaging Center at Caltech. MRI is a non-optical imaging technique that derives image contrast from the protons in water. Because MRI is non-optical, the entire volume of opaque specimens can be imaged throughout. The brain surfaces were generated using a generalized marching cube algorithm and rendered with Amira softwarc.

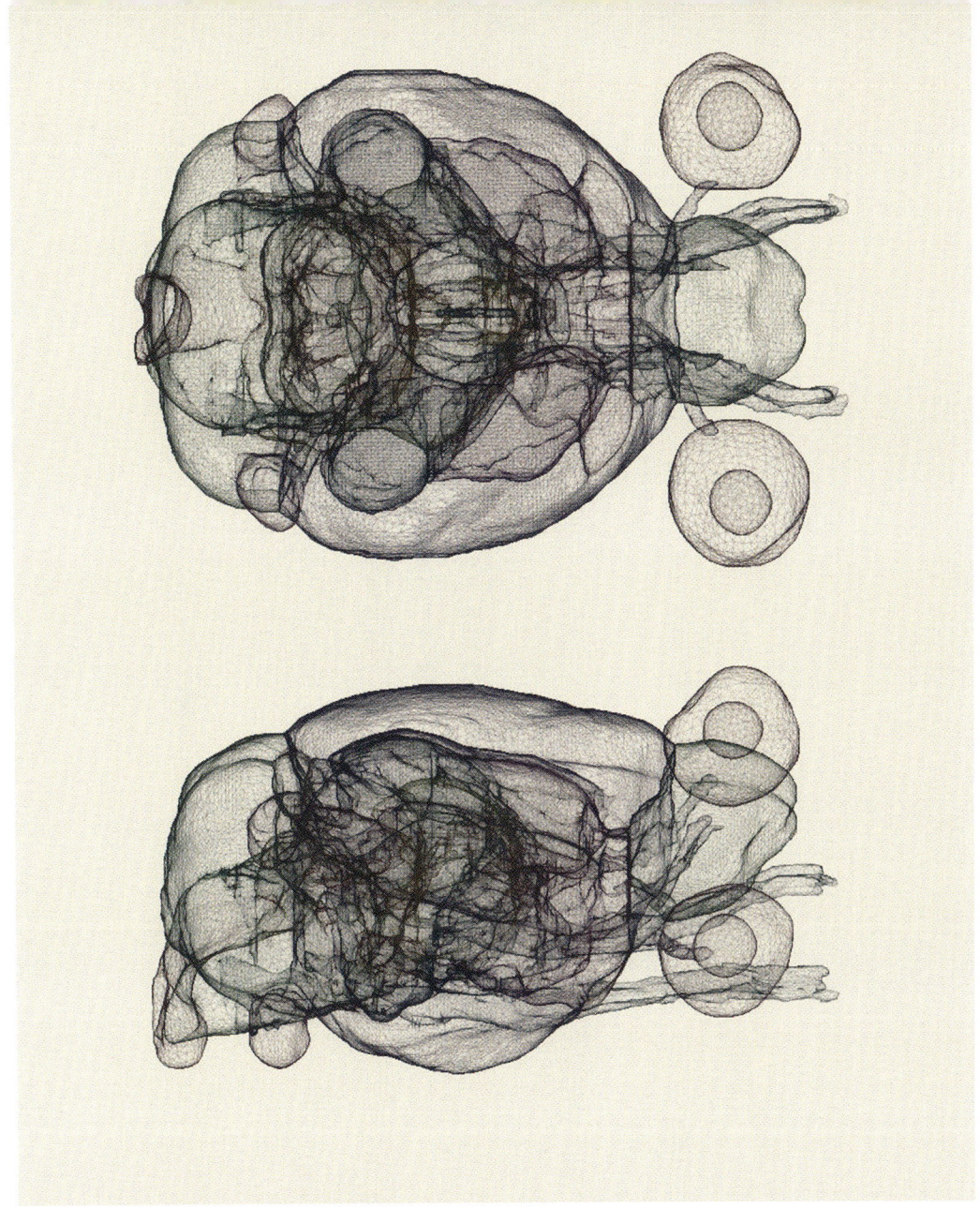

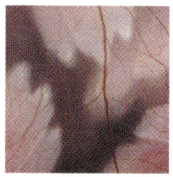

Michael Schenk and Robert Gray

White Rat Fetus, *Rattus norvegicus albinus,* 2003

Natural science photograph; Canon-Kodak CDS150 with Canon 180 mm F3.5 Macro lens and 2× extender

University of Mississippi Medical Center, Jackson, Mississippi, United States

The close-up photograph of a white rat fetus includes the uterine wall which is still attached while the chorion membrane has been removed. The vascular transparent amniotic membrane surrounding both the fetus and umbilical cord is exposed. A gestation period of 21–23 days is normal for this species. The fetus shown in this photograph is approximately 20 days post-conception. This photograph was produced for use in high school, college biology, and zoology reference materials. The photograph complements other illustrations that depict the gross anatomical view of the reproductive system of a pregnant female rat.

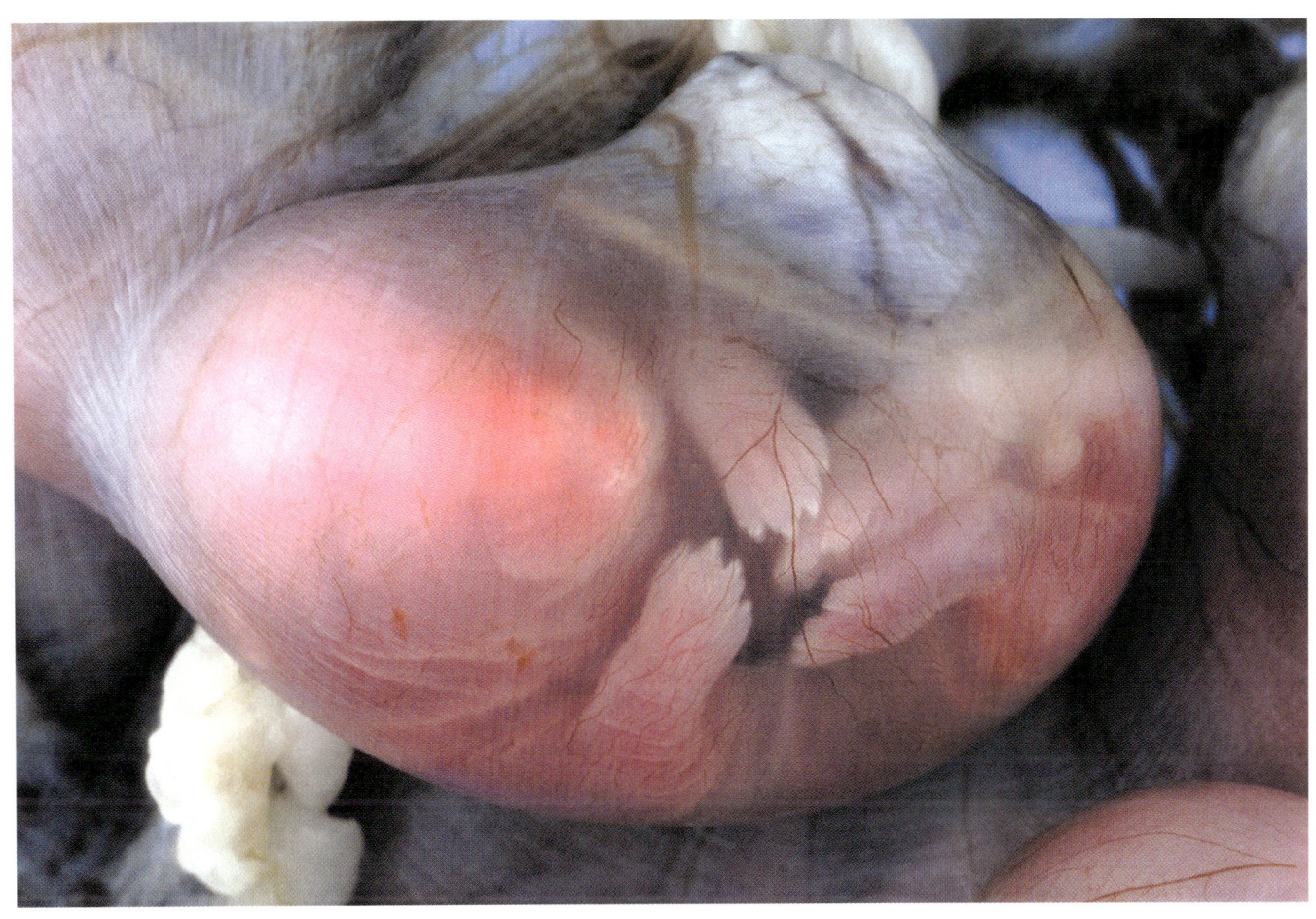

93

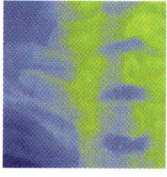

Henry Schleichkorn

Digitally Colored Radiograph

Radiograph; Digital capture Canon Mark II DS Camera

Custom Medical Stock Photo, Chicago. Illinois, USA

A radiographic imaging system produces monochromatic images. Consequently these grayscale images, when used for non-clinical applications such as public relations and marketing purposes, might be considered dull and uninteresting. In this photograph of a healthy human chest, the boney skeleton, lungs and the shadow of the heart are all visible. In this radiograph, various regions have been colorized selectively to create more visual interest and drama.

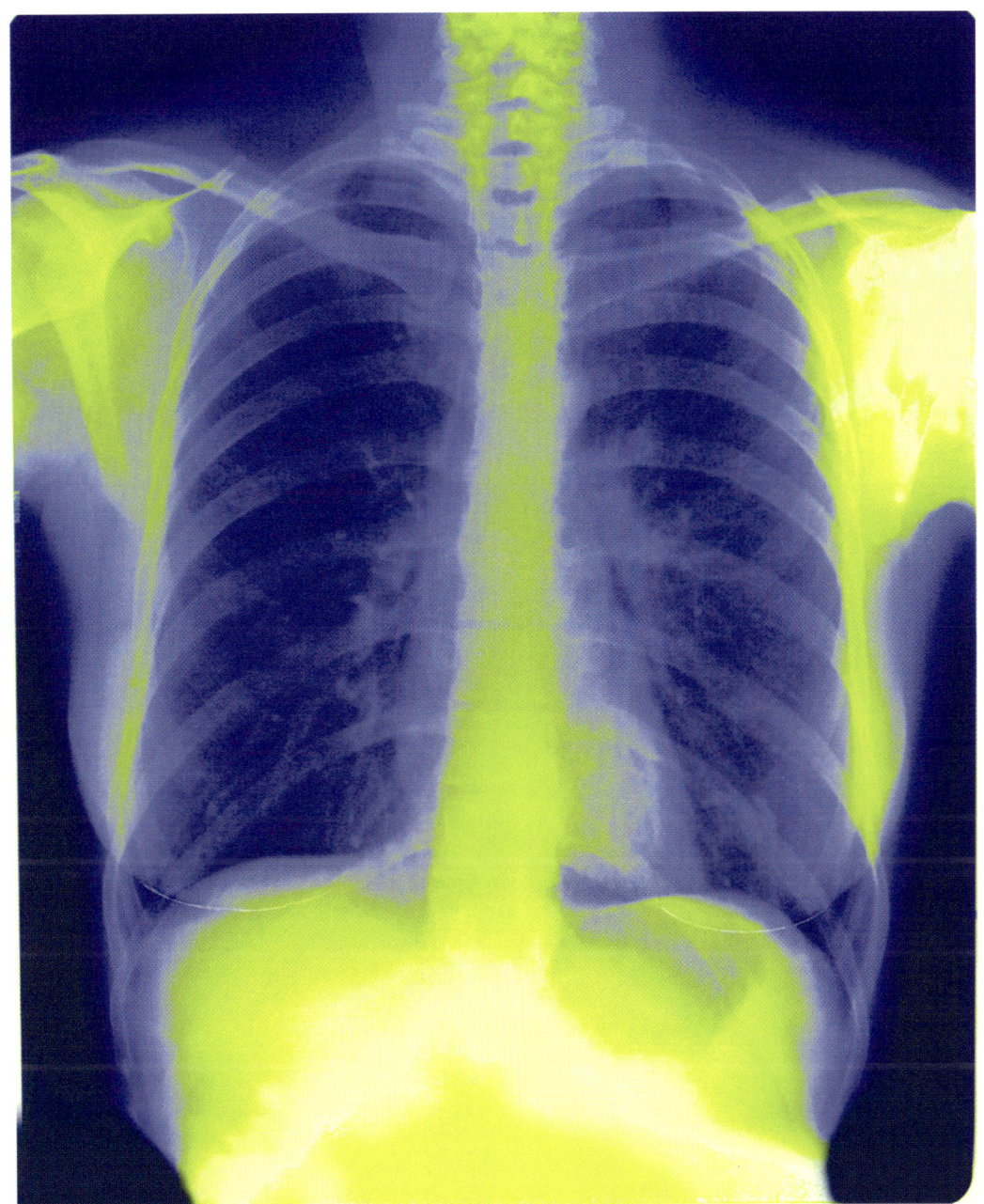

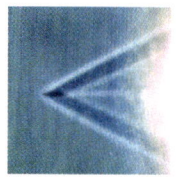

Gary S. Settles

Instantaneous Schlieren Image of Rifle Discharge, 2004

High-speed schlieren photograph; initial capture Pentax 67 medium-format camera; 120mm color negative roll film; 4-microsecond flash illumination; Image was obtained using the Penn State full-scale schlieren optical system laboratory

Pennsylvania State University, Gas Dynamics Laboratory, University Park, Pennsylvania, United States

This schlieren photograph captured the instantaneous act of firing a .30-06 high-powered rifle. The supersonic bullet and spherical muzzle blast are visualized as a direct consequence of the schlieren system. The Penn State lab has a unique schlieren optical system that uses a 2 μ 3-meter mirror, which was required to take the photograph. This facility is part of Penn State's Gas Dynamics Laboratory. The shooter is Lori J. Dodson.

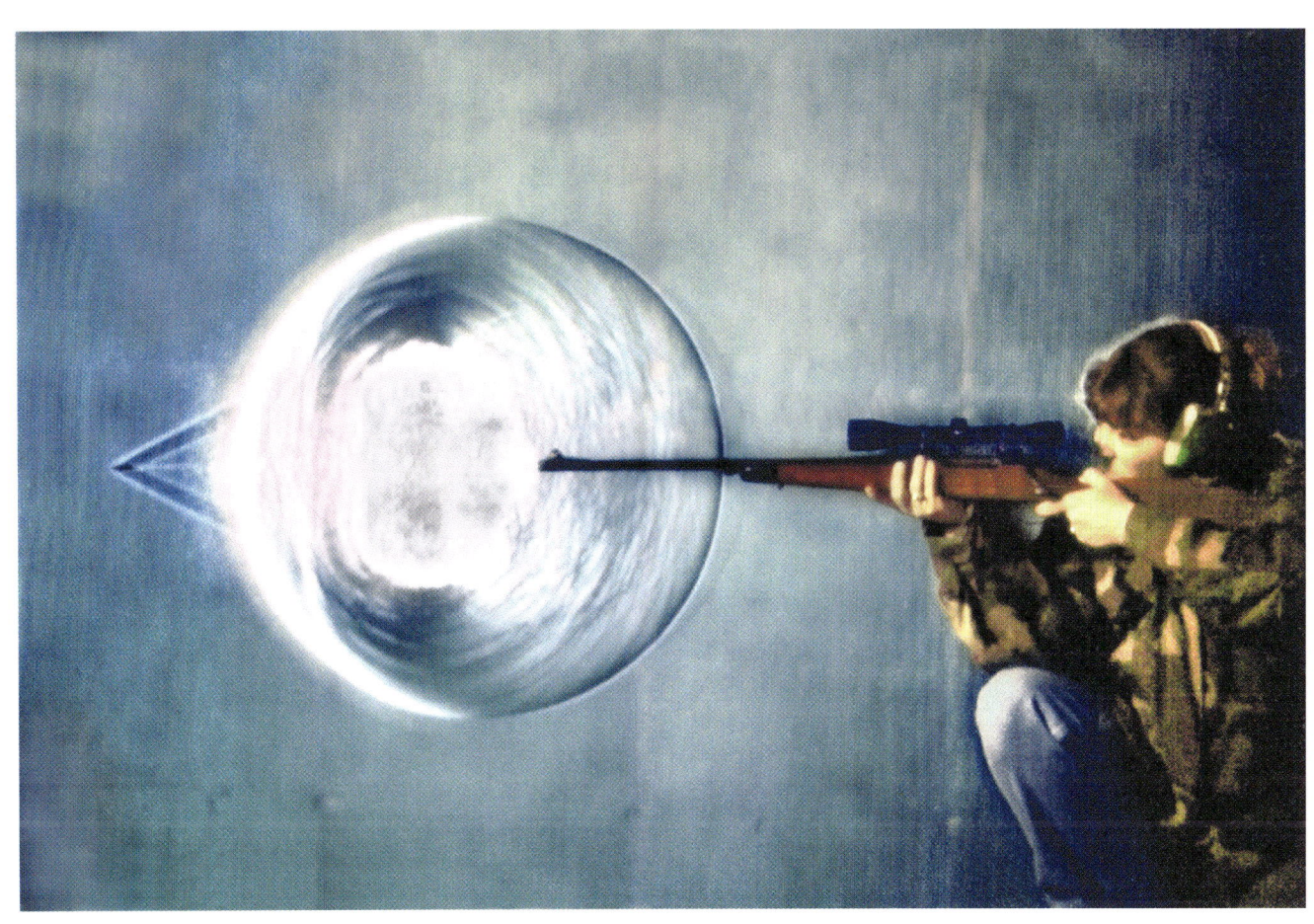

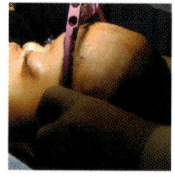

Mary Spano

Placing the RED Device, 2007

Medical photograph; Nikon D200 digital camera

The Institute of Reconstructive Plastic Surgery, New York University School of Medicine, New York, New York, United States

In this photograph, the RED (rigid external distraction) device is used in the LeFort III mid-face advancement surgery procedure. This procedure is performed on patients with craniofacial deformities such as Crouzon, Apert, and Pfeiffer Syndromes, which effects the fusion of skull bones. The RED Device is an external halo-like metal frame that is attached to the skull, assisting with the gradual movement and growth of new bone to treat the facial abnormality. In this photograph, the surgeons are viewing a 3D rendering of a CAT scan performed on the patient just prior to surgery. This helps guide the surgeons in making the precise cuts in the bone (osteotomies) and the positioning of the device, which will hold the bones in place during the advancement process. With the advancement of the mid-face region there are often noticeable improvements in the airway function, eye protection, dental occlusion, and speech. Additionally, the appearance of the patient will often be improved.

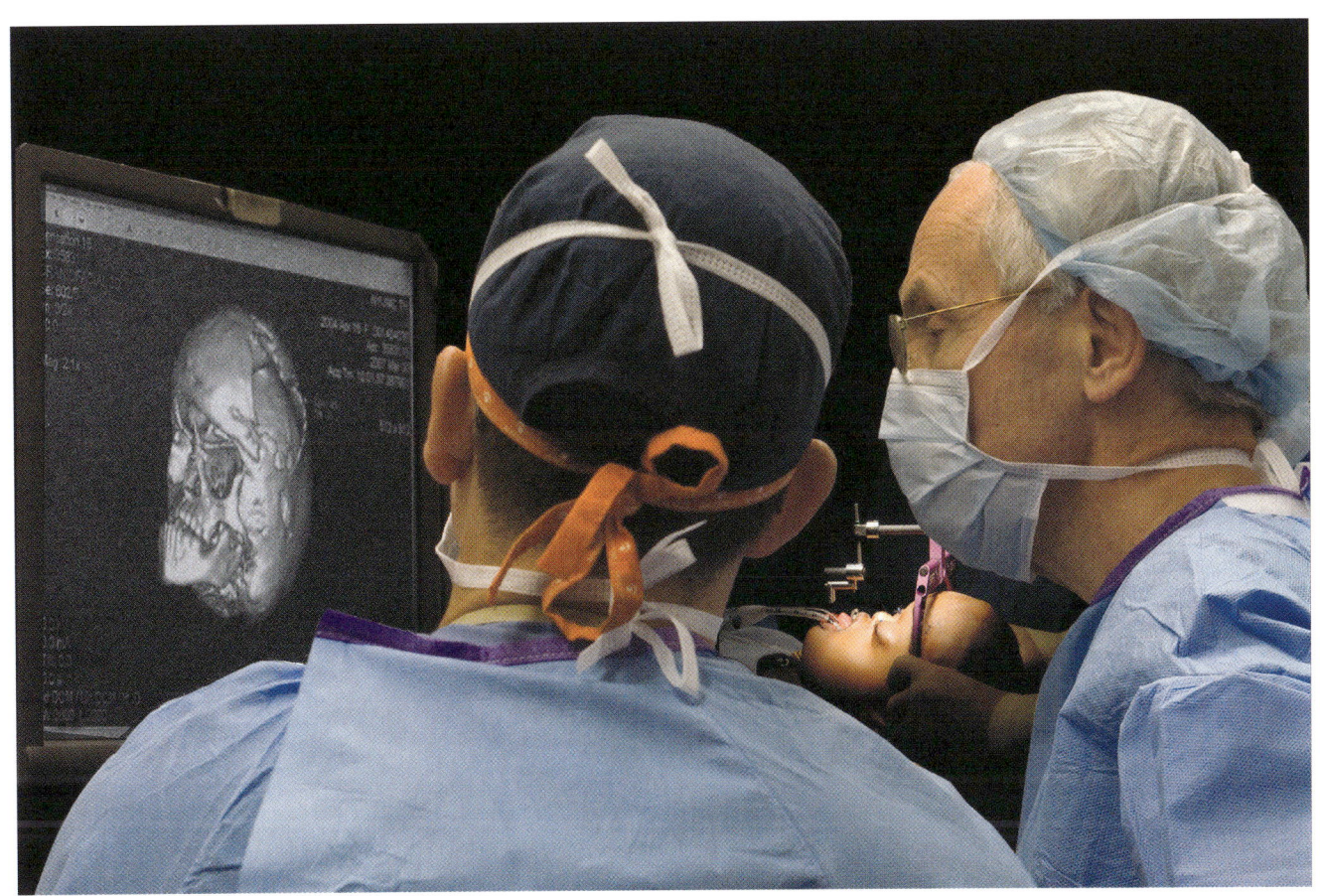

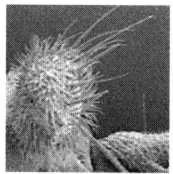

Scott Streiker

Fruit Fly, *Drosophila melanogaster*, 2007

Scanning electron photomicrograph; magnification approximately ×120 at capture

Nanoscale Engineering Science and Technology Laboratory (NEST), University of Dayton Research Institute, Dayton, Ohio, United States

The sample in this photograph was prepared for photography using critical point drying, which was followed by sputter coating using gold to provide electrical conduction. For samples to be evaluated in SEM, they cannot contain any moisture and their surfaces must reflect electrons. After dehydration, sputter coating creates a reflective and conductive surface. This image was created as part of student training on a high-resolution scanning electron microscope (HRSEM) for a graduate biology course taught at the University of Dayton. In the photograph, the compound eyes, antennae and mouth-parts are visible.

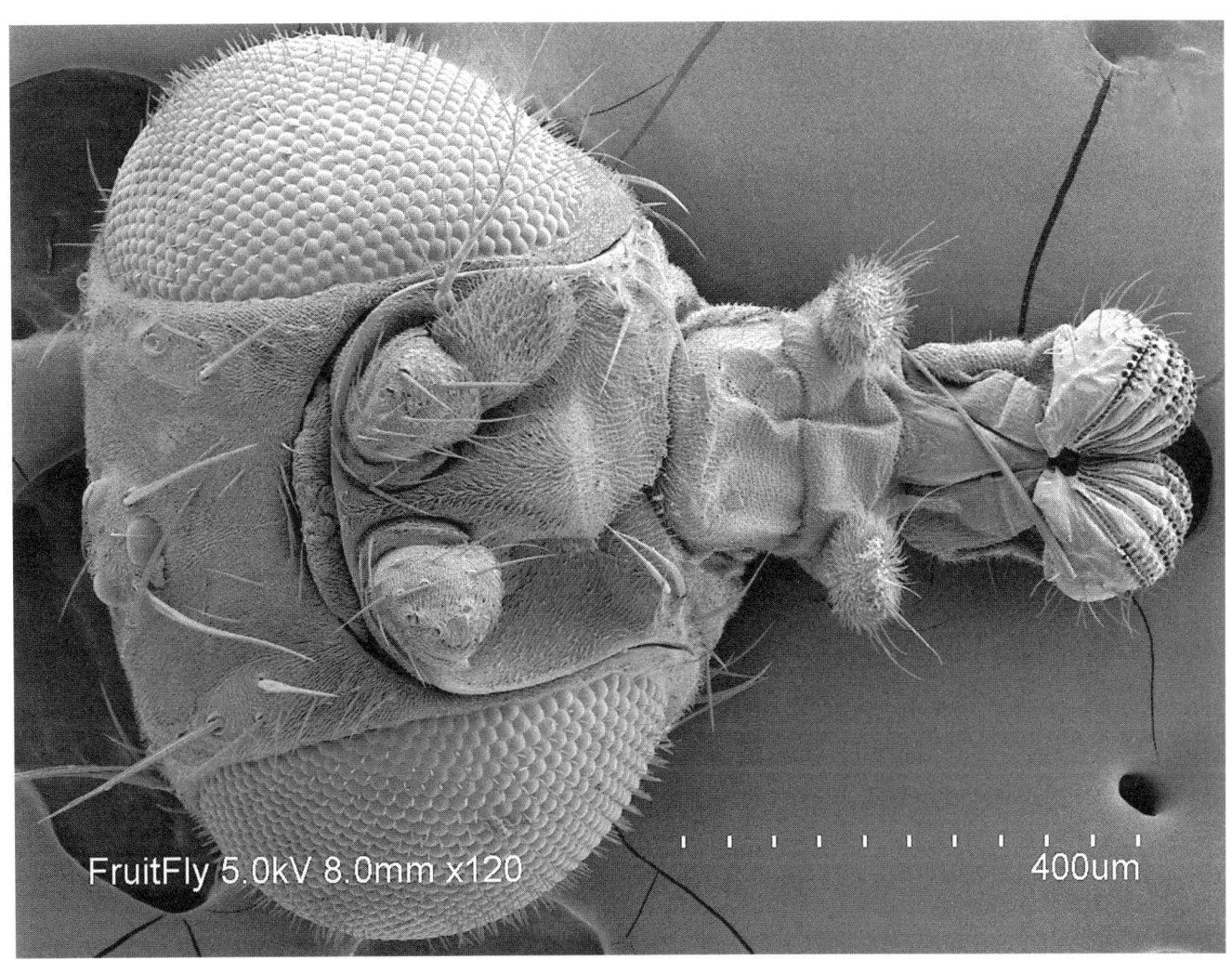

FruitFly 5.0kV 8.0mm x120   400um

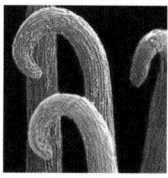

Viktor Sykora

Agrimonia eupatorium Seed, 2008

Scanning electron photomicrograph; JEOL 6380 scanning electron microscope; post-capture digital colorization

First Faculty of Medicine, Charles University, Prague, Czech Republic

Agrimony is a perennial flowering plant that is in the same botanical family as the rose. It exhibits medicinal anti-inflammatory and diuretic properties. Parts of these plants contain large quantities of tannins and flavonoids, as well as smaller amounts of essential oils and vitamin C. This photograph shows the upper part of an Agrimony seed with its hook-like protrusions. These hooks along with the burrs, spine, and bristle structures, assist in seed dispersal through a process known as epizoochory, where animals inadvertently transport plant seeds or fruits because the seed becomes temporarily attached on the host's fur.

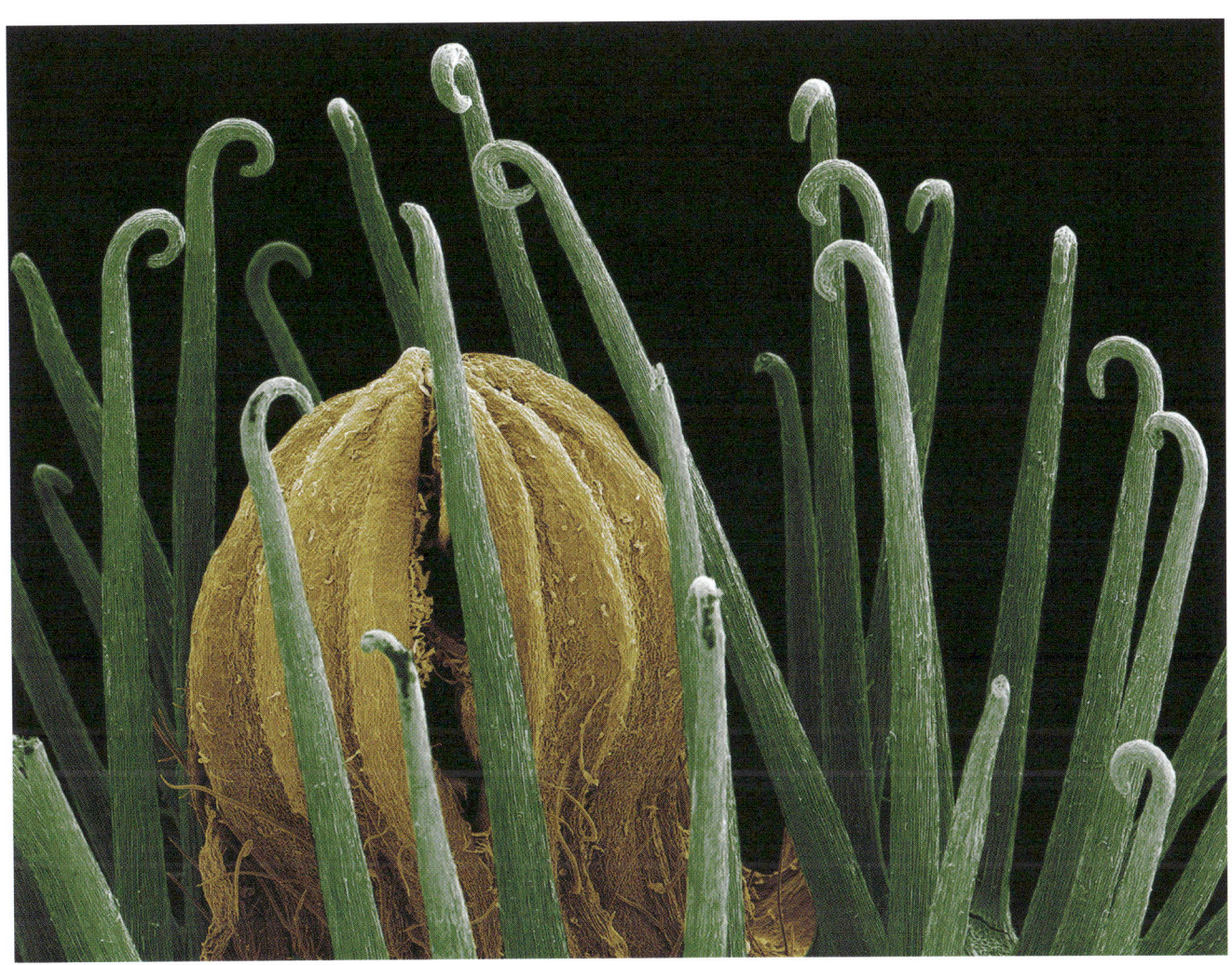

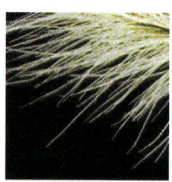

Viktor Sykora

Clematis recta Seed, 2007

Natural science photograph; Nikon D80

First Faculty of Medicine, Charles University, Prague, Czech Republic

Clematis recta 'Purpurea' is a non-climbing variety of Clematis that produces white flowers and grows to approximately three feet tall. The long, furry projection of the plant's seed is visible under low magnification. These structures enable the seed to be carried by the wind for new plant germination—a dispersal method called anemochory.

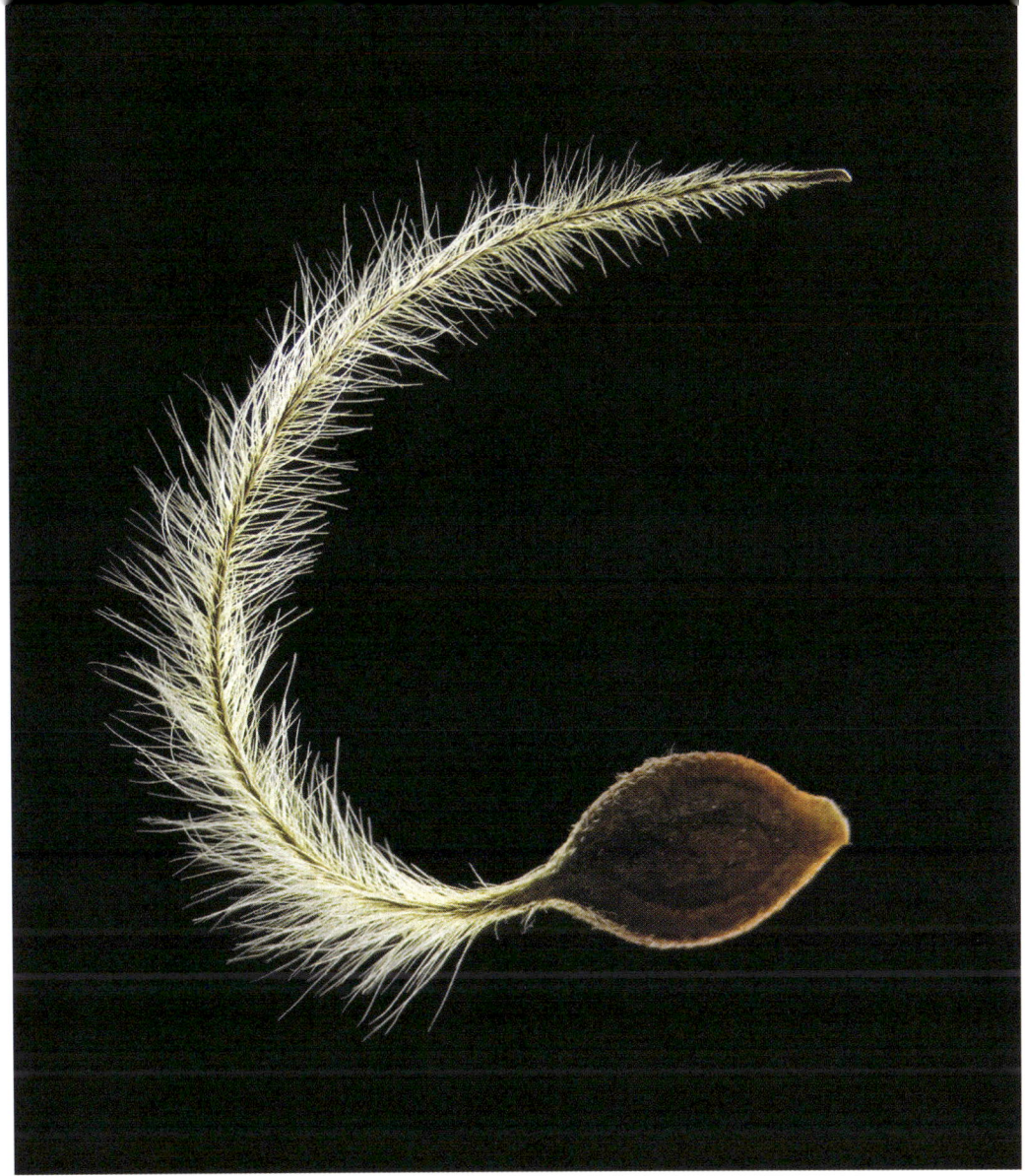

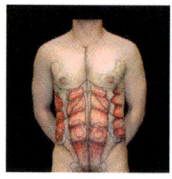

David Teplica

Frustration, Logic, and Resolution, 2008

Composite Medical Photograph; original print; 5 × 11 foot mural using archival pigments on cotton paper; Nikon Cool-Pix 990 camera; Rigidly standardized full-torso peri-operative sequence

Plastic Surgery, University of Chicago Hospitals, Chicago, Illinois, United States

This composite photograph is comprised of many standardized full-torso photographs showing a male patient's high-definition circumferential liposuction, including "before" views at top; "preoperatively marked" at center; and "postoperative" results at bottom. The image series allows for accurate and quantifiable analysis of anatomic changes. The markings shown at center were made directly on the patient before surgery. Their color-coding is as follows: black for anatomic landmarks and boney boundaries; green contour rings that designated areas of breast formation; red for muscular volume; blue contour rings delineated areas of fatty redundancy; blue stippling showed fatty regions that were to be aspirated; and purple marks defined incision and excision locations. The patient entered into the 4 to 6 hour surgery with all the marks intact to guide the surgical process of bodily proportioning. The final result sequence was photographed 15 months post-operatively, clearly indicating the subject's heightened torso definition.

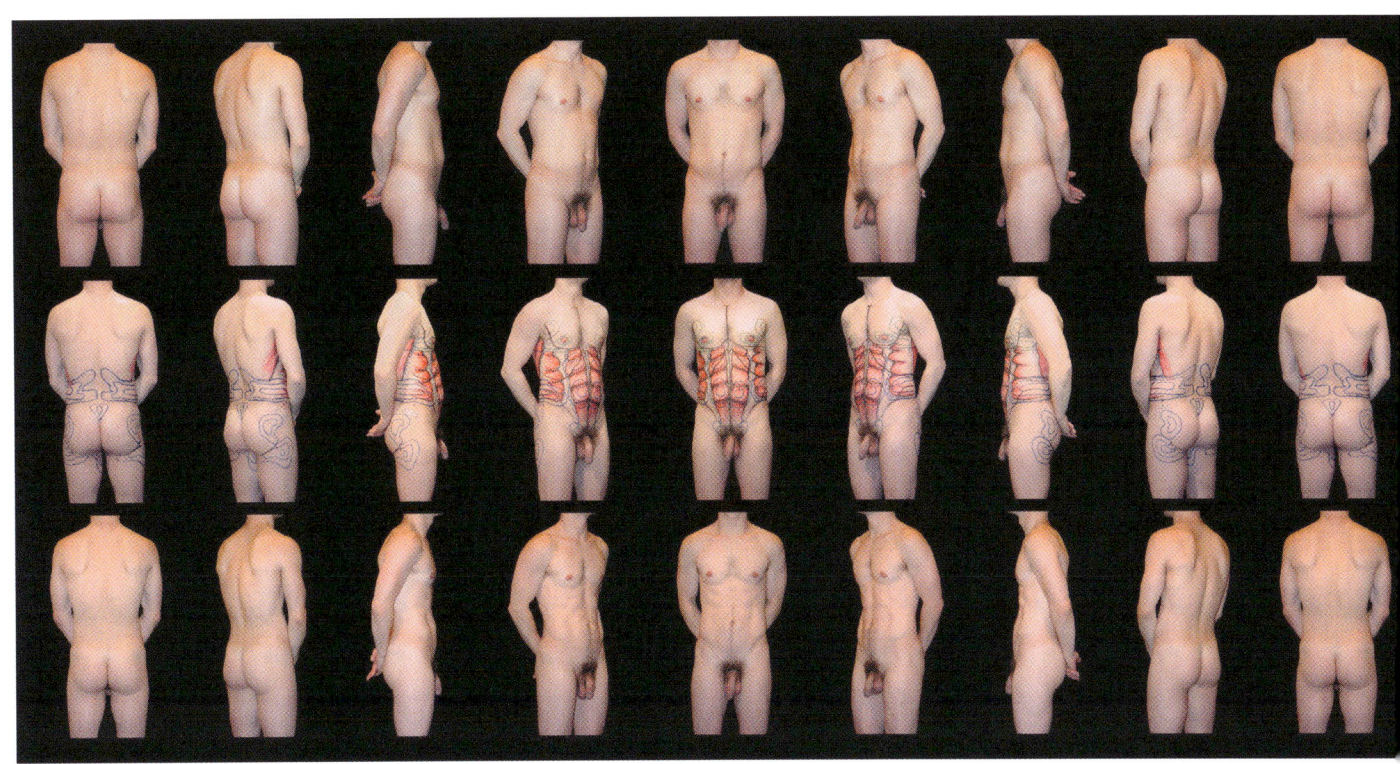

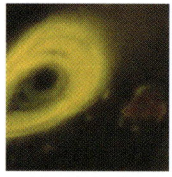

Bob Turner

Tetracycline in Bone and Muscle, 1978

Photomicrograph; magnification approximately ×240 at capture;
fluorescence photomicroscope; Kodak Ektachrome EL [ASA 400] film

The Scripps Research Institute, BioMedical Graphics, La Jolla, California, United States

In certain conditions, the introduction of the drug tetracycline into a subject's diet can facilitate the direct observation of bone cell growth. When examined using fluorescence illumination, bone cells will clearly demonstrate relative daily growth as "rings," seen here in the yellow circular structure of this canine bone. Muscle tissue in this sample appears green under fluorescence. Continued daily observation enables delineation of fine detail from one day to the next, and illustrates variations in growth rate as diet is changed in content and/or quantity. This data can then be used to help prescribe the best diet to use to foster bone growth, which in turn, promotes healing.

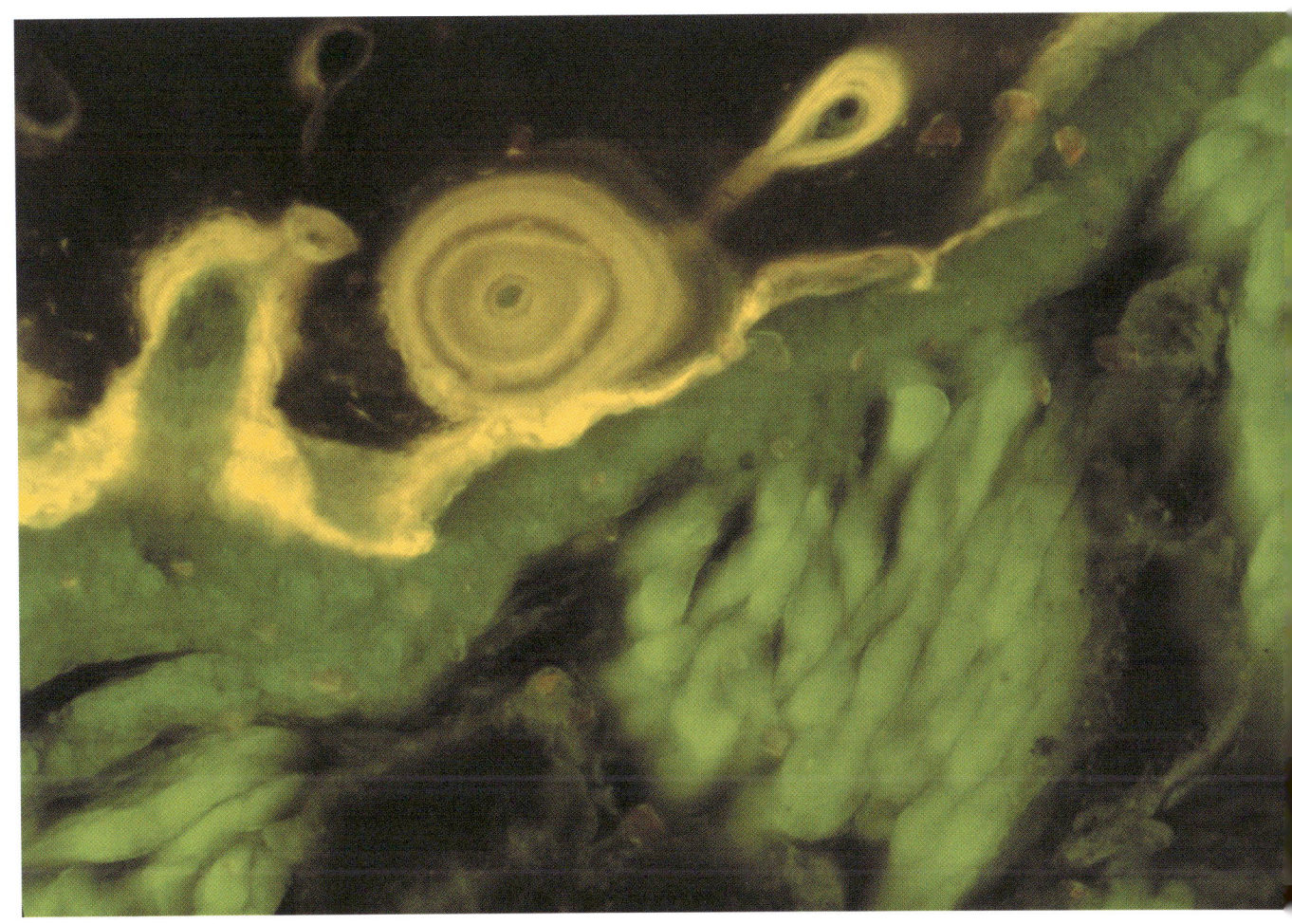

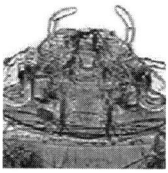

David Walker

Water Beetle in Transmitted Near Infrared Energy, 2005

Photomicrograph; Zeiss microscope with a Zeiss 1× Plan Achromatic objective;
video still frame image captured with 'Snappy' video capture box;
four images recorded and stitched to extend field of view

Huddersfield, West Yorkshire, United Kingdom

When using transmitted visible light for examination, the exoskeleton of some prepared insect microscopy slides can be nearly opaque, however when examining the same field using near infrared wavelengths, data is more readily observed to reveal details otherwise invisible to the human eye. This image was made using hobby-grade imaging equipment including a student microscope, a homemade near infrared LED lamp, and a domestic black and white security camera for image capture. This accounts for the small image size. The slide was prepared at a slide-mounting course with materials and techniques supplied by Northern Biological Supplies.

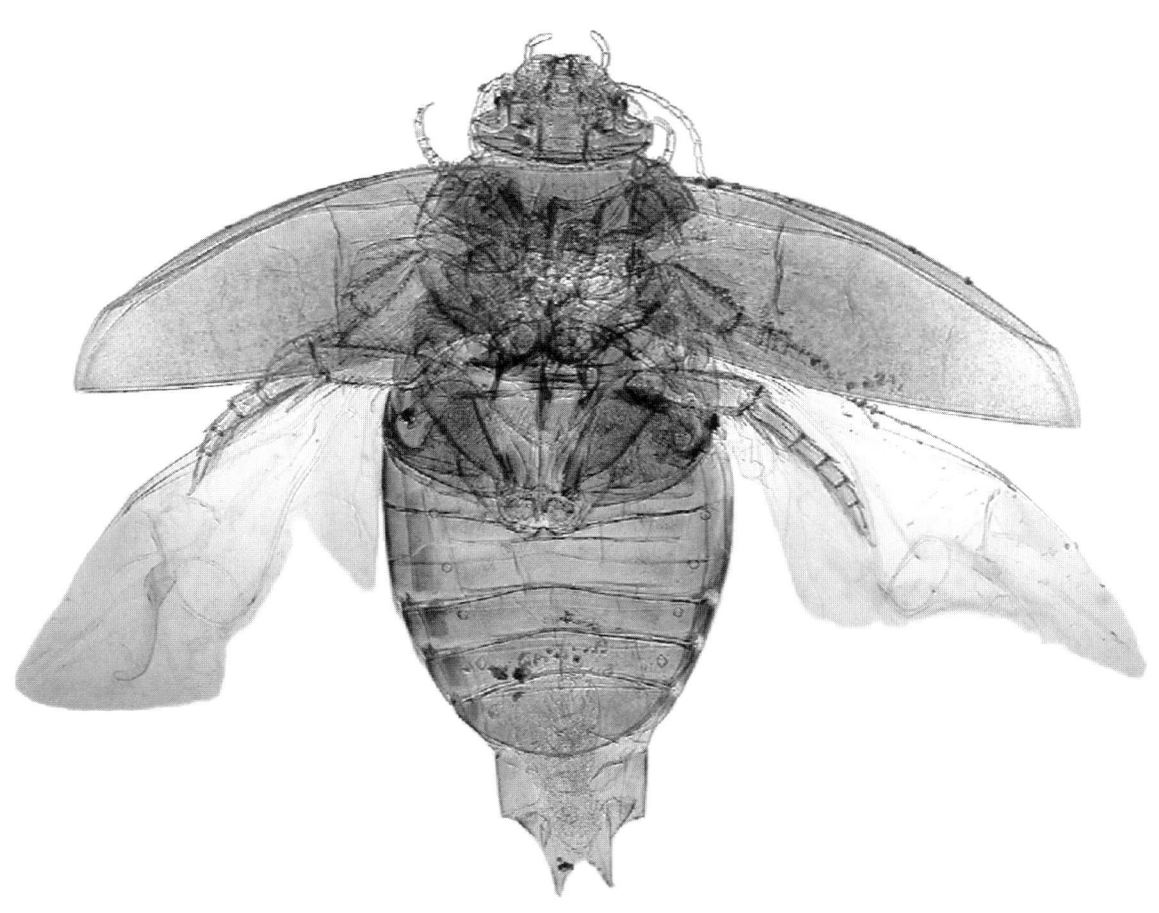

111

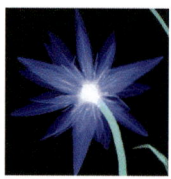

Jim Wehtje

Electra Water Lily, 2006

Digitally-edited radiograph; Faxitron X-ray equipment; Grenz rays;
.5 mm source size; mammography film; post capture colorization

Jim Wehtje Photography, Rochester, New York, United States

This X-ray or radiographic image reveals the internal structure of an Electra water lily, *Nymphaea* 'Electra.' This image was created from approximately 70 individual radiographs exposed onto mammography film from an exposure of low energy X-rays, also called Grenz rays, using a .5 mm source size. The numerous individual images were then stitched together using Adobe PhotoShop CS® software. Colorizing was done after stitching.

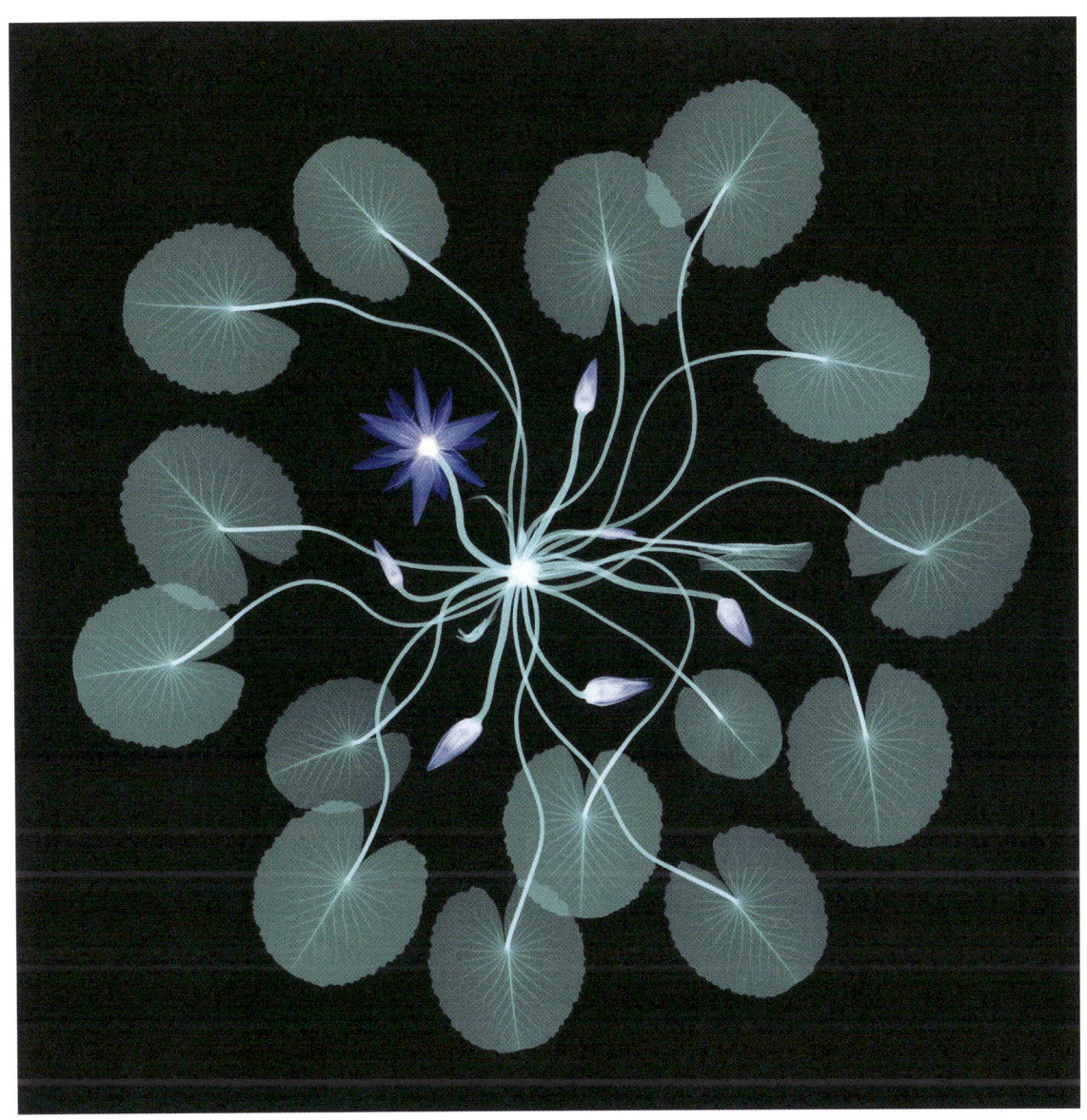

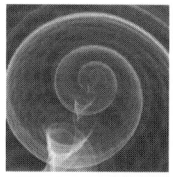

Jim Wehtje

Tun Study, 2005

Digitally-edited radiograph; Faxitron X-ray equipment; Grenz rays;
.5 mm source size; mammography film; post capture colorization

Jim Wehtje Photography, Rochester, New York, United States

These three radiographic views reveal the structure of a banded tun shell, *Tonna sulcosa*. Banded tuns are mollusks native to Indo-Pacific waters. Their external shell markings are typically white with brown spiral ridges. Each image was exposed using a single piece of mammography film and the composite was created post capture. The radiographs were exposed using low energy x-rays, also called Grenz rays, using a .5 mm source size.

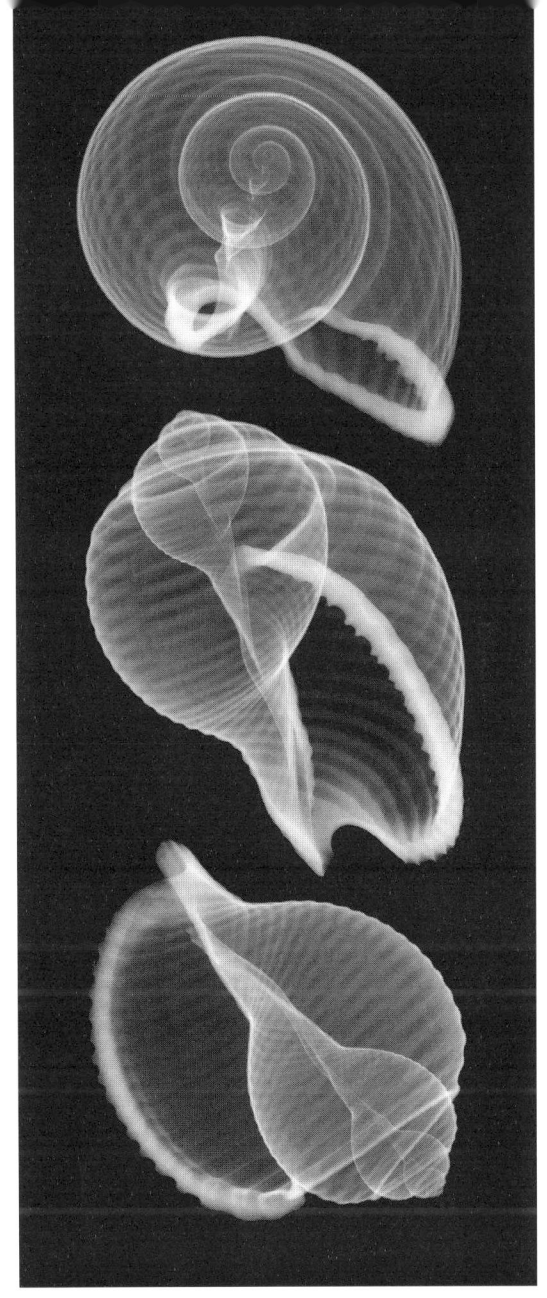

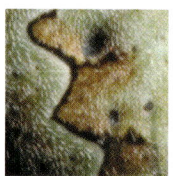

Paul Whitten

Giant Lichen Orb Weaver Spider, *Araneus bicentenarius,* 2005

Photomacrograph; direct digital capture; electronic flash

New York Eye and Ear Infirmary, Department of Medical Photography, New York, New York, United States

Orb weavers comprise a very large family of spiders including several hundred species in North America alone. The giant lichen orb weaver spider, *Araneus bicentenarius,* was first described in 1888 by Henry C. McCook—a well-known naturalist and vice president of the Academy of Natural Sciences located in Philadelphia. There are few species of orb weavers with green abdominal patterns such as this one. Its size, beautiful coloration, and impressive web structure make it a privilege to locate when chanced upon. This specimen was photographed in-situ in Casco, Maine.

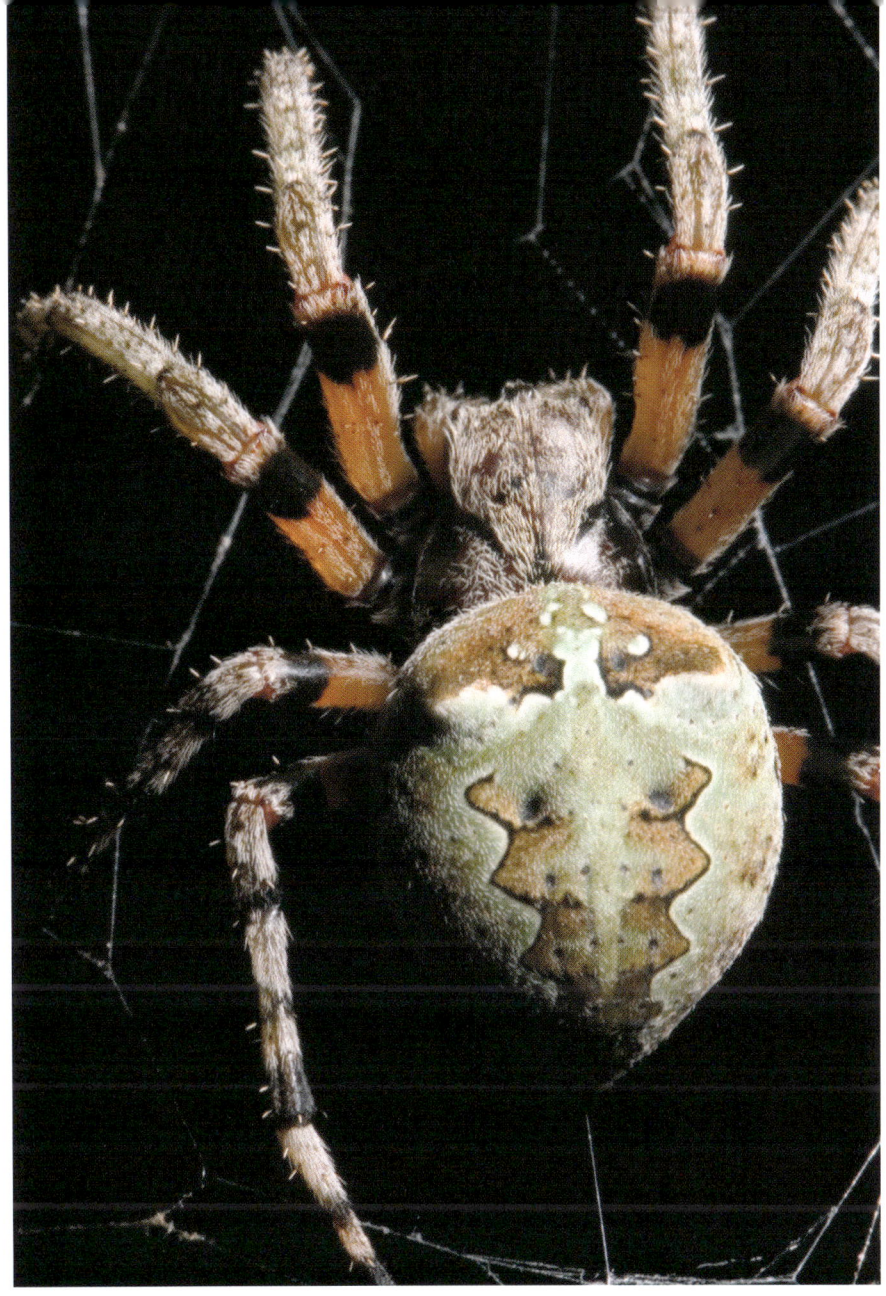

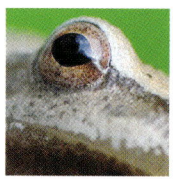

Paul Whitten

Male Spring Peeper, *Hyla crucifer,* 2006

Photomacrograph, direct digital capture

New York Eye and Ear Infirmary, Department of Medical Photography, New York, New York, United States

The chorus of the spring peeper, *Hyla crucifer,* is one of the first signs of spring in the central and eastern United States and Canada. This small tree frog measures from 1.9 to 3.5 cm long. Its high-pitched ascending whistle produced by males can be heard over a long distance. Peepers are found in grassy lowlands and wooded areas near ponds, swamps, and temporarily flooded areas. They are generally nocturnal, emerging at night to feed on insects, spiders, and other small invertebrates. Like the wood frog, spring peepers can survive being almost entirely frozen while hibernating during the winter months. This frog was photographed in Hunter, New York.

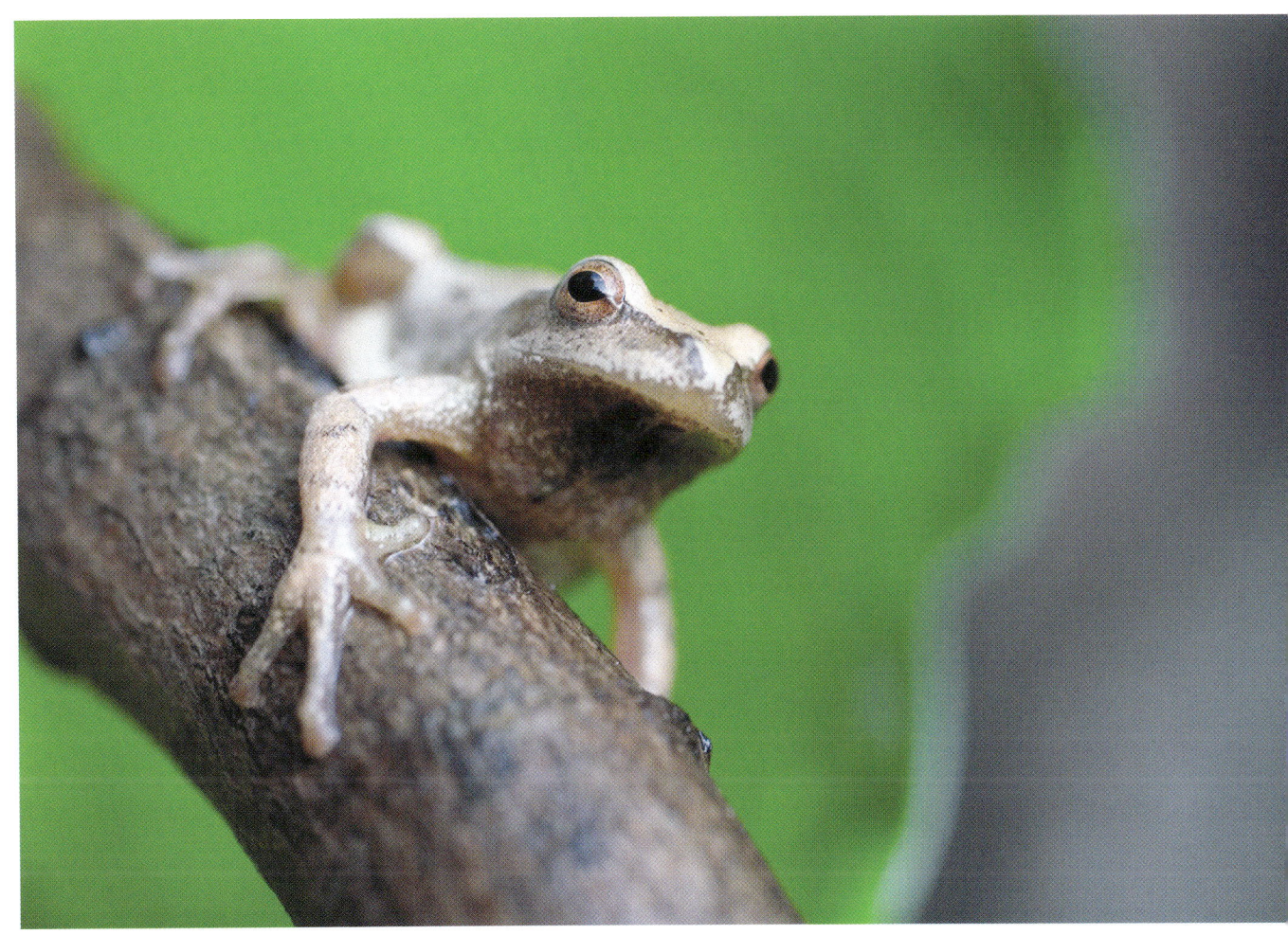

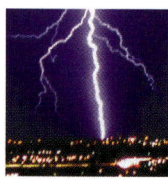

Kent Wood

Hexed, 1993

Night time landscape photograph; Yashica Mat TLR camera; tripod mounted;
120mm color transparency film

Albuquerque, New Mexico, United States

This photograph recorded a classic example of lightning's randomly dynamic symmetry.
Multiple cloud to ground lighting bolts emanate from two opposing regions of a
cumulonimbus cloud over Tucson, Arizona in 1993. This time-exposure photograph
captured the enormous energy that a single convective thunderstorm can release
during a violent electronic storm in the southwest.

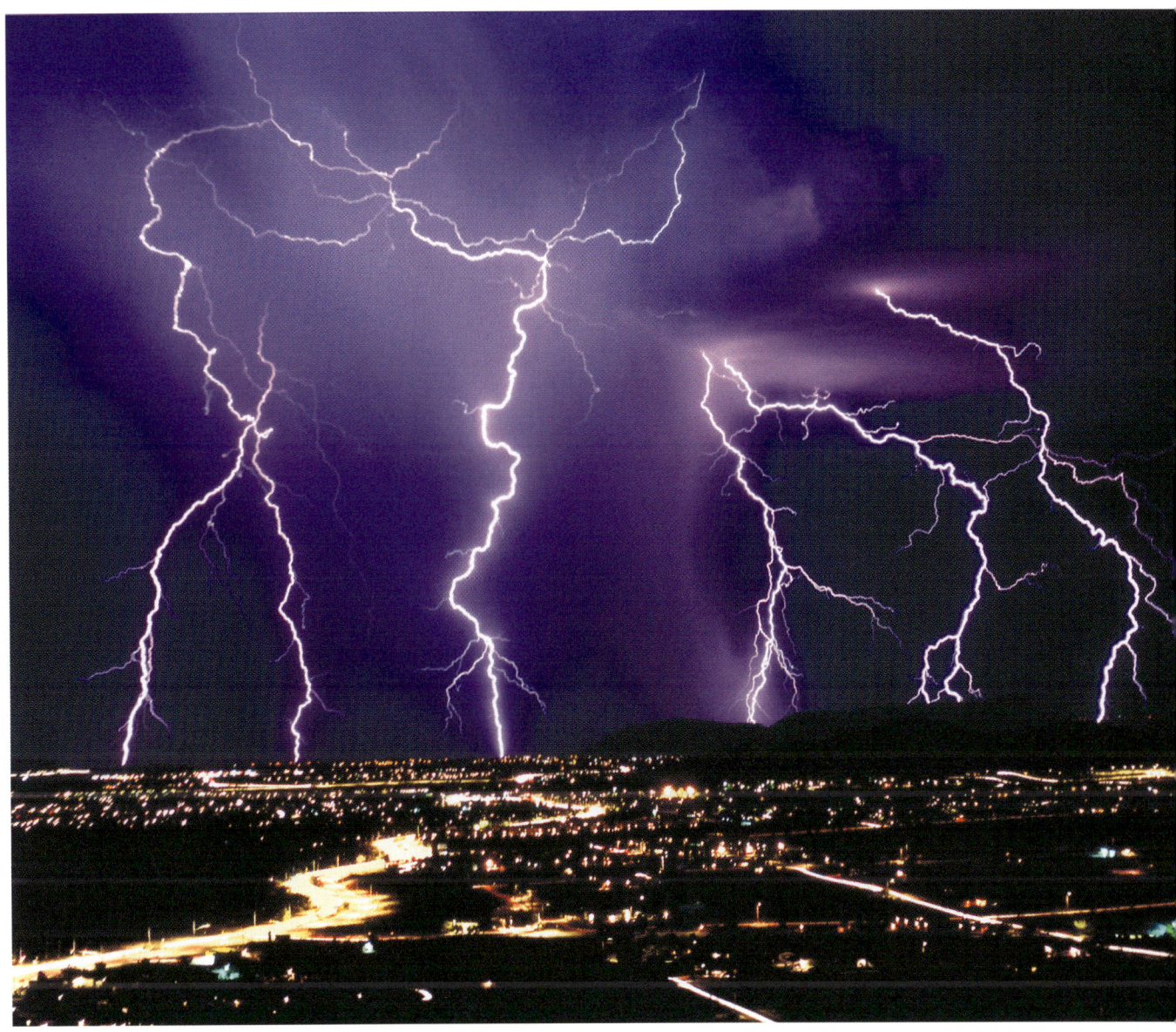

The Judges

A. Becquer Casaballe

Fotomundo, Buenos Aires, Argentina

A. Becquer Casaballe is the editor of *Fotomundo,* a highly respected photography magazine published in Buenos Aires, Argentina. He is also a professor of documentary photography at the University of Buenos Aires and author of the book *Imágenes del Río de la Plata. Crónica de la fotografía rioplatense 1840–1940.* He has presented conferences, courses, and seminars in Argentina, Uruguay, Brazil, Puerto Rico, and France. His photographs have been exhibited in the Museum of Fine Arts of Houston, Texas; the Musée de la Photographie de Chaleroi, Belgium; the International Center of Photography, New York, the Museu de Arte Contemporânea de São Paulo, Brazil; and the Maison de l'Amérique Latine, Paris, France, among others.

Dennis di Cicco

Sky & Telescope, Cambridge, Massachusetts, USA

Dennis di Cicco is the Senior Editor of *Sky & Telescope* magazine published in Cambridge, Massachusetts. His early hobbies of photography and astronomy quickly developed during his teenage years and they have since played a central role in his life—working for 34 years on the editorial staff of *Sky & Telescope.* Dennis has had a long-time affection for making pictures of the night sky and is interested in the history of scientific photography. His award-winning photographs have appeared in hundreds of books and magazines, including *National Geographic, Life, Time,* and *Newsweek.* His work was also shown at the inaugural display of Kodak's Professional Photographer's Showcase at Epcot Center in Florida.

William W. DuBois

Rochester Institute of Technology, School of Photographic Arts and Sciences, Rochester, New York, USA

William W. DuBois has worked at the Rochester Institute of Technology since 1974 when he accepted a faculty appointment at the School of Photographic Arts and Sciences. Professor DuBois has held a variety of positions in the school during his 30-plus-year career, including his service as the program chair of four different degree programs. In his most recent appointment, he was the administrative chair of Photographic Arts division, which directed the BFA degree programs in advertising photography, fine art photography, photojournalism, visual media, and the imaging arts master's degree program. As a professor at the school, he specializes in architectural photography. He is the co-owner and operator of Images & Ideas, a business that was started in 1986 which provides full-service architectural photography for architects, interior, designers, and contractors. He graduated from Ohio University in 1967 with a BFA in commercial photography and also earned his master's in education from Bowling Green State University in 1974.

Julieanne Kost

Adobe Systems, Inc., San Jose, California, USA

Julieanne Kost joined Adobe in 1992 where she serves as the Senior Digital Imaging Evangelist. At Adobe, she has continually developed cutting-edge digital skills as a consequence of her immersion in myriad photographic projects. Her expertise spans digital imaging and illustration, while her role at Adobe often includes customer education, product development, and market research. She is a frequent contributor to several publications, a speaker at numerous design conferences and tradeshows, and a teacher at distinguished photography workshops and fine art schools around the world. She is a passionate photographer and combines her background in psychology in creating her artwork. She is the author behind *Window Seat: The Art of Digital Photography and Creative Thinking,* and the Photoshop Fundamentals and Advanced Photoshop Techniques training DVDs published by Software Cinema.

Michael J. McNamara

New York, New York, USA

Michael J. McNamara was most recently the Executive Technology Editor for *Popular Photography* magazine published in New York, serving as an editor at that the magazine for 17 years. Mike earned his BS degree in imaging and photographic technology from Rochester Institute of Technology School of Photographic Arts and Sciences in 1990.

Lennart Möller, M.D.

Karolinksa Institutet, Stockholm, Sweden

Lennart Möller is a Professor and a Doctor of Medicine at the Karolinska Institutet located in Stockholm, Sweden. Professor Möller is the Deputy chairman of the Lennart Nilsson Award foundation who presents a prize annually to extraordinary image makers in science. Additionally, he was the Editor of *Images in Science* (imagesinscience.com), Karolinska University Press, published in 2003.

Bonnie Stutski

Smithsonian, Washington, DC, USA

Bonnie Stutski currently serves as the Senior Photography Editor for *Smithsonian* magazine. In this role, she oversees the conceptualizing, assigning, directing, researching, editing, and the selection of photography that will be used to illustrate Smithsonian's feature articles and photo essays, which often explore a variety of national and international topics. Bonnie has been a Photography Editor at *Smithsonian* since 1995. Her prior experience in the fields of photography and publishing spans more than 30 years and includes editing for National Wildlife Federation Books, National Geographic Society, and Time-Life books. She is a member of NANPA (North America Nature Photography Association), ASPP (American Society of Picture Professionals), and ASMP (American Society of Media Photographers).

The Organizers

Professor Andrew Davidhazy is a faculty member in the Imaging and Photographic Technology Department, which is one of seven programs of study offered in the School of Photographic Arts and Sciences at Rochester Institute of Technology. He has been a faculty member for more than 30 years and specializes in high speed, photoinstrumentation, ballistic, forensic, infrared, ultraviolet, and various other scientific and technical aspects of photography. He is also active in the exploration of technical imaging methods for aesthetic purposes. He has lectured and exhibited widely and his photographs and writings have been published in numerous books, articles, and journals including *Popular Photography, American Photo, Industrial Photography, Camera,* etc. He is a recognized expert in the area of scanning photography, especially panoramic photography and peripheral portraiture. He was the Inaugural Kodak Visiting professor to Australia in 1992 and has also been an exhibitor and guest lecturer at photographic and educational institutions in Argentina, Sweden, France, Brazil, and many other societies and organizations worldwide. He has been the recipient of the RIT Eisenhart Award for Outstanding Teaching and is a Fellow of the Society for Imaging Science and Technology as well as the International Society for Optical Engineering.
http://people.rit.edu/andpph

Professor Michael Peres has served as the chair of the Biomedical Photographic Communications department at the Rochester Institute of Technology since 1989. As a member of the teaching faculty in the School of Photographic Arts and Sciences for 22 years, his expertise includes photography using magnified imaging systems as well as biomedical photography and related technologies. Peres has been active in

publishing most of his career and recently served as editor-in-chief for the revision of the *Focal Encyclopedia of Photography*, fourth edition. He has also presented numerous papers and imaging-related workshops all over the United States, as well as in Sweden, Tanzania, the Netherlands, Germany, and Australia, that investigate topics such as digital imaging at the light microscope and the production of QuickTime VR movies. He has been a member of BioCommunications Association since 1978 and is also a member of the Ophthalmic Photographers' Society. Some of his current professional activities include chair of the Lennart Nilsson Award Nominating Committee, Stockholm, Sweden and one of the coordinators for the annual RIT Big Shot, http://www.rit.edu/cias/bigshot. In April 2003, he was awarded one of the RIT Eisenhart Awards for Outstanding Teaching as selected by the faculty. He has also been twice awarded the Gitner Prize presented by the RIT College of Imaging Arts and Sciences, and he was the recipient of 2007 Louis B. Schmidt Award presented by the BioCommunications Association. Michael holds a master's degree in instructional technology and bachelor's degrees in biology and biomedical photographic communications. He is also a registered biological photographer.
http://people.rit.edu/mrppph

Acknowledgements

It has been our experience that large projects typically start slowly and then they take on a life of their own. More importantly we have also learned that to achieve all of a project's objectives requires the help of an entire community. With the experiences gained from the first exhibition that we organized in 2002, we were acutely aware that this project would again require vital collaborations if we were going to achieve the results we envisioned.

In the context of this brief statement, we cannot begin to express the heartfelt gratitude we feel towards all of the various contributors and supporters who made this exhibition and catalogue possible. From the beginning, at discussions with colleagues both at RIT and in the industry, we received encouragement and, significantly, financial help that allowed us to keep moving ahead with the expectation of a successful outcome

The decision to produce another installation of the *Images from Science* exhibition occurred after a chance meeting with Julieanne Kost, of Adobe, who was visiting RIT in February 2007. That meeting resulted in discussions with Chitra Mittha, the Photoshop Senior Product Marketing Manager for Adobe Systems, Inc., who expressed interest in supporting the exhibition. Building on Chitra's encouragement and Adobe's significant pledge, in August 2007 we proceeded to launch the project and started moving ahead with the numerous organizational, promotional and other details related with mounting the exhibition.

We are excited with the ultimate outcome and would like to recognize the following *Images from Science 2* partners for their financial support towards the production of this exhibition. Kenny Patterson, National Sales Manager, Zeiss MicroImaging, Inc., the College of Imaging Arts and Sciences FEAD grant committee, and Tim

Saur of Durst Image Technology, US, LLC. Their sponsorship allowed us to produce very high quality exhibition prints and an impressive catalogue. We also thank RIT Cary Graphic Arts Press for their endorsement and willingness to again take on the publishing of the catalogue. In particular we would like to recognize Amelia Hugill-Fontanel, Production Editor at the Press. Her oversight and continual assistance enabled us to produce this excellent catalogue a second time.

We would also like to thank Dr. Joan Stone, Dean of the College of Imaging Arts and Sciences, for extending her personal support and endorsement on behalf of the College.

Moving the large files our contributors produced electronically could simply have been accomplished using a CD and postal services but instead the RIT Computer Science House, a special interest floor of the Residence Life at RIT, created and made available a wonderful and secure FTP site for us to use. This process of image transfer was used by more than 75% of the contributors.

The opportunity to be part of this project was all we had to offer Martin Scott, the former Director of Scientific Photography at Eastman Kodak, who volunteered to write the guest essay for the exhibition. Martin's career spanning many decades in scientific photography made him uniquely qualified to write this overview.

Once the images were submitted, image selection became the work for our select panel of judges who were charged with identifying the images that are included in this exhibition. Our world-renowned panel included Julieanne Kost of Adobe Systems, Inc.; A. Becquer Casaballe of Fotomundo; Dennis di Cicco of Sky & Telescope; William W. DuBois of the RIT School of Photographic Arts and Sciences; Michael J. McNamara; Lennart Möller, M.D., of Karolinska Institute; and Bonnie Stutski of Smithsonian. We thank them all for their donation of time and technical, as well as visual, expertise.

There are also many people who worked out of sight but whose contributions were also indispensable. Peter Gabak was instrumental in working with our collaborators ensuring the sponsorships were handled properly. Thanks go as well to Marnie Soom, book designer at Cary Graphic Arts Press, who made everything look great for this impressive collection.

A.D. and M.P.

Sponsors

We would like to thank the following sponsors who made *Images from Science 2* possible:

Adobe, Inc.

Carl Zeiss MicroImaging, Inc.

Durst Image Technology US, LLC

Lennart Nilsson Award Foundation

Rochester Institute of Technology

RIT Cary Graphic Arts Press

RIT College of Imaging Arts and Sciences

RIT Computer Science House

RIT School of Photographic Arts and Sciences

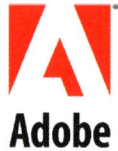 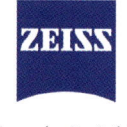 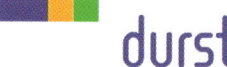 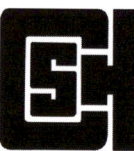

About the *Images from Science* Exhibition

During the summer of 2001, the idea to produce an exhibition that featured images of scientific photography was suggested. The goal of that exhibition was to showcase work produced by photographer/scientists whose work was perhaps virtually unknown to the general public. At the time, digital photography was rapidly displacing film technology as the major imaging technology used in science and the Internet had become—seemingly overnight—the principal communication tool for many. Additionally, Professors Davidhazy and Peres were both personally interested in explorations of the interface of the arts and sciences and they were aware of several initiatives such as the Nikon Small World exhibition where scientific images were being shown principally for aesthetic reasons. Starting only with their idea, they proceeded to create the exhibition using experimental methods to overcome the obstacles they encountered along the way. After eighteen months, which included the production of a 4-color catalogue, the first *Images from Science* exhibition opened on October 12, 2002 in the School of Photographic Arts and Sciences Gallery at the Rochester Institute of Technology. It was displayed at RIT until December 2002. Following that showing, the exhibition traveled to twenty three other venues spanning ten states in the U.S., and five countries internationally. In June 2008, the show was retired. Following is the complete list of where the *Images from Science* exhibition was displayed:

Academia Film Olomouc
Univerzita Palackeho at Olomouci
Olomouc, Czech Republic

Academic Hospital Groningen
Rijks University
Groningen, Netherlands

The Academic Medical Centre
Amsterdam, Netherlands

Allen Chapman Gallery
University of Tulsa
Tulsa, Oklahoma, USA

Arizona Health Sciences Library
University of Arizona
Tucson, Arizona, USA

Biological Sciences Building
University of Puerto Rico, Mayaguez Campus
Mayaguez, Puerto Rico

Discovery Science & Technology Center of Bethlehem
Bethlehem, Pennsylvania, USA

The European Conference on Visual Perception
A Coruña, Spain

Gahlberg Gallery
College of DuPage
Glen Ellyn, Illinois, USA

Harvard University
Boston, Massachusetts, USA

Johnson & Johnson World Headquarters
New Brunswick, New Jersey, USA

Karolinska Institutet-Astra Pharmaceuticals
Stockholm, Sweden

Lennart Nilsson Conference
Karolinska Institutet
Stockholm, Sweden

Louisiana State University Health Sciences Center
The Medical Center Library Gallery
Shreveport, Louisiana, USA

New York Hall of Science
Brooklyn, New York, USA

Peggy Notebaert Nature Museum
Chicago, Illinois, USA

Rijnstate Hospital
Arnhem, Netherlands

RIT Inn & Conference Center
Rochester Institute of Technology
Rochester, New York, USA

SPIE-International Society for Optical Engineering Conference
San Diego, California, USA

Swedish National Medical Fair
Gothenberg, Sweden

Tower Fine Arts Gallery
Bausch & Lomb World Headquarters Gallery
Rochester, New York, USA

University of Dublin
Dublin, Ireland